W9-CNA-866

Gun Control

30036008910935

Gun Control

Angela Valdez

SERIES CONSULTING EDITOR
Alan Marzilli, M.A., J.D.

CHELSEA HOUSE
PUBLISHERS
A Haights Cross Communications Company

Philadelphia

This book is intended to serve only as a general introduction to the political and legal issues surrounding gun control. It is not intended as legal advice. If you have a legal problem, you should consult a licensed attorney who is familiar with the laws and procedures of your jurisdiction.

CHELSEA HOUSE PUBLISHERS

VP, NEW PRODUCT DEVELOPMENT Sally Cheney
DIRECTOR OF PRODUCTION Kim Shinners
CREATIVE MANAGER Takeshi Takahashi
MANUFACTURING MANAGER Diann Grasse

Staff for GUN CONTROL

EDITOR Patrick M.N. Stone
PRODUCTION EDITOR Jaimie Winkler
PHOTO EDITOR Sarah Bloom
SERIES AND COVER DESIGNER Keith Trego
LAYOUT 21st Century Publishing and Communications, Inc.

A Haights Cross Communications ✔ Company

http://www.chelseahouse.com

First Printing

1 3 5 7 9 8 6 4 2

Library of Congress Cataloging-in-Publication Data

Valdez, Angela.
    Gun control/Angela Valdez.
        p. cm.—(Point/counterpoint)
Includes bibliographical references and index.
    ISBN 0-7910-7371-8 HC   0-7910-7507-9 PB
    1. Gun control—United States—Juvenile literature. 2. Firearms ownership—
United States—Juvenile literature. [1. Gun control. 2. Firearms ownership.]
I. Title. II. Point/counterpoint (Philadelphia, Pa.)
HV7436 .V35 2002
323.4'3—dc21

                                                2002152055

CONTENTS

Introduction
Alan Marzilli, M.A., J.D.
Durham, North Carolina

The debates presented in POINT/COUNTERPOINT are among the most interesting and controversial in contemporary American society, but studying them is more than an academic activity. They affect every citizen; they are the issues that today's leaders debate and tomorrow's will decide. The reader may one day play a central role in resolving them.

Why study both sides of the debate? It's possible that the reader will not yet have formed any opinion at all on the subject of this volume—but this is unlikely. It is more likely that the reader will already hold an opinion, probably a strong one, and very probably one formed without full exposure to the arguments of the other side. It is rare to hear an argument presented in a balanced way, and it is easy to form an opinion on too little information; these books will help to fill in the informational gaps that can never be avoided. More important, though, is the practical function of the series: Skillful argumentation requires a thorough knowledge of *both* sides—though there are seldom only two, and only by knowing what an opponent is likely to assert can one form an articulate response.

Perhaps more important is that listening to the other side sometimes helps one to see an opponent's arguments in a more human way. For example, Sister Helen Prejean, one of the nation's most visible opponents of capital punishment, has been deeply affected by her interactions with the families of murder victims. Seeing the families' grief and pain, she understands much better why people support the death penalty, and she is able to carry out her advocacy with a greater sensitivity to the needs and beliefs of those who do not agree with her. Her relativism, in turn, lends credibility to her work. Dismissing the other side of the argument as totally without merit can be too easy—it is far more useful to understand the nature of the controversy and the reasons *why* the issue defies resolution.

The most controversial issues of all are often those that center on a constitutional right. The Bill of Rights—the first ten amendments to the U.S. Constitution—spells out some of the most fundamental rights that distinguish the governmental system of the United States from those that allow fewer (or other) freedoms. But the sparsely worded document is open to inter-pretation, and clauses of only a few words are often at the heart of national debates. The Bill of Rights was meant to protect individual liberties; but the needs of some individuals clash with those of society as a whole, and when this happens someone has to decide where to draw the line. Thus the Constitution becomes a battleground between the rights of individuals to do as they please and the responsibility of the government to protect its citizens. The First Amendment's guarantee of "freedom of speech," for example, leads to a number of difficult questions. Some forms of expression, such as burning an American flag, lead to public outrage—but nevertheless are said to be protected by the First Amendment. Other types of expression that most people find objectionable, such as sexually explicit material involving children, are not protected because they are considered harmful. The question is not only where to draw the line, but how to do this without infringing on the personal liberties on which the United States was built.

The Bill of Rights raises many other questions about individ-ual rights and the societal "good." Is a prayer before a high school football game an "establishment of religion" prohibited by the First Amendment? Does the Second Amendment's promise of "the right to bear arms" include concealed handguns? Is stopping and frisking someone standing on a corner known to be frequented by drug dealers a form of "unreasonable search and seizure" in violation of the Fourth Amendment? Although the nine-member U.S. Supreme Court has the ultimate authority in interpreting the Constitution, its answers do not always satisfy the public. When a group of nine people—sometimes by a five-to-four vote—makes a decision that affects the lives of hundreds of millions, public outcry can be expected. And the composition of the Court does change over time, so even a landmark decision is not guaranteed to stand forever. The limits of constitutional protection are always in flux.

These issues make headlines, divide courts, and decide elections. They are the questions most worthy of national debate, and this series aims to cover them as thoroughly as possible. Each volume sets out some of the key arguments surrounding a particular issue, even some views that most people consider extreme or radical—but presents a balanced perspective on the issue. Excerpts from the relevant laws and judicial opinions and references to central concepts, source material, and advocacy groups help the reader to explore the issues even further and to read "the letter of the law" just as the legislatures and the courts have established it.

It may seem that some debates—such as those over capital punishment and abortion, debates with a strong moral component—will never be resolved. But American history offers numerous examples of controversies that once seemed insurmountable but now are effectively settled, even if only on the surface. Abolitionists met with widespread resistance to their efforts to end slavery, and the controversy over that issue threatened to cleave the nation in two; but today public debate over the merits of slavery would be unthinkable, though racial inequalities still plague the nation. Similarly unthinkable at one time was suffrage for women and minorities, but this is now a matter of course. Distributing information about contraception once was a crime. Societies change, and attitudes change, and new questions of social justice are raised constantly while the old ones fade into irrelevancy.

Whatever the root of the controversy, the books in POINT/COUNTERPOINT seek to explain to the reader the origins of the debate, the current state of the law, and the arguments on both sides. The goal of the series is to inform the reader about the issues facing not only American politicians, but all of the nation's citizens, and to encourage the reader to become more actively involved in resolving these debates, as a voter, a concerned citizen, a journalist, an activist, or an elected official. Democracy is based on education, and every voice counts—so every opinion must be an informed one.

In this volume, Angela Valdez covers the debate over gun control. The wording of the Second Amendment is open to debate: "A well-regulated Militia, being necessary to the security of a free State, the right of the people to keep and bear Arms, shall not be infringed." But what is a militia? Who are "the people"? What is meant by "Arms"—and keeping and bearing them? How absolute did the Framers intend "shall not be infringed" to be? And does this mean that people can use guns for any purpose, or just for maintaining a citizen militia?

While courts have debated the constitutional question, society has struggled with some important matters of public policy: Is violent crime attributable to gun ownership, or are guns necessary for self-defense? Who should bear responsibility for the thousands of firearm deaths each year? This book raises these and other important questions about a crisis facing the nation.

The Politics of Gun Control

In 1968, in the space of about two months, the United States lost two men who had been voices for peace and social change during a decade of tension and turbulent clashes. Black civil rights leader Martin Luther King, Jr. was shot and killed April 4, 1968, as he stood on the balcony of the Lorraine Motel in Memphis, Tennessee. James Earl Ray, a career criminal, was convicted of King's murder.

Then, on June 5, 1968, Robert F. Kennedy, a presidential candidate and brother of slain President John F. Kennedy, was gunned down at the Ambassador Hotel in Los Angeles. Kennedy, 42, had just declared his victory in the crucial California Democratic Primary. He died a day later. The gunman, Sirhan B. Sirhan, was captured at the scene and later convicted of murder.

People gather in Colorado to protest the National Rifle Association (NRA) and its support of almost unlimited gun ownership. Former Supreme Court Chief Justice Warren Burger accused the NRA of having too much influence on politics.

These violent and public assassinations catalyzed a sudden national obsession with gun violence in the United States. The policy debate over gun control took a central position in the U.S. media and has yet to fade from the political landscape.

The issue of gun control occupies a singular position in U.S. politics. On this subject, the same left and liberal advocates who might lobby in the name of free speech for the right to burn the flag or the freedom not to say the Pledge of Allegiance may also oppose the freedom of individuals to own guns. Conservatives who might argue against First Amendment protections for pornography or oppose the rigorous separation of church and state can become staunch defenders of the Bill of Rights when the Second Amendment right to own firearms is discussed prominently alongside freedom of speech and of religion.

The debate summons emotional images of our frontier past, a time when firearms helped earlier Americans form a new country. The icons of U.S. heroism, superiority, and even glamour rely heavily on the symbolic power of the gun: the American Revolutionary soldier, the self-reliant pioneer, the cavalier gangster or cowboy, the intrepid private detective, and the policeman.

The anti–gun control position is bolstered by the individualistic tradition in U.S. political philosophy. In this view of politics, each person's rights and value supersede the needs and beliefs of citizens as a group, the government, or the nation. (This self-based belief system is also at the root of the reluctance in the United States to agree on nationalized health care or identification cards.)

In recent years, mass shootings and high numbers of inner-city deaths caused by firearms fueled demands for increasing gun control, and grass-roots citizens' groups organized protests and campaigns to pressure their representatives in state houses and on Capitol Hill. Although ideology and policy dominated the discussion, many observers saw the issue becoming more of a political tool than a subject for reform. Elected officials from both major parties have used their opposition to or support for gun control to win elections. According to the Center for Responsive Politics (*www.opensecrets.org*), opponents of gun control contributed more than $4.3 million during the 1999–2000 campaign cycle. About 90 percent of the money went to Republican groups and candidates. Gun control advocates spent more than $476,000 on donations, with most of their money helping Democrats. In addition to promoting candidates that favor their political goals, gun control and gun rights groups try to influence legislation in Congress. To this end, advocacy groups spend what they can afford on lobbying Congress: Major gun control groups spent $420,000 on lobbying in 2000. Gun rights organizations spent almost $6.7 million.

> **How large a role does money play in politics?**
>
> **Should money play as large a role as it does?**
>
> **If not, then how can its role be reduced?**

The money for these donations comes from a small number of large organizations on either side of the debate. For those opposed to gun control, the National Rifle Association (NRA) has long been the main representative. The groups supporting gun control are more numerous and include the Brady Center to Prevent Handgun Violence and the Violence Policy Center.

Current Regulations on Firearms

The Second Amendment, in its entirety, states the following:

> A well-regulated Militia, being necessary to the security of a free State, the right of the people to keep and bear Arms, shall not be infringed.

Current U.S. gun control laws attempt to reduce violence by barring civilians from owning certain high-risk military weapons, including machine guns and some semi-automatic assault weapons, and by prohibiting certain groups from owning guns. These groups include felons, children, and people with diminished mental capacity. The law requires background checks on licensed sales of firearms and requires manufacturers to imprint each firearm with a serial number.

Does it make sense to ban certain types of gun if almost all guns are potentially lethal?

Where the Debate Stands

Advocates of gun control believe lives will be saved if the government makes it even harder for people to own firearms. They advocate waiting periods on gun purchases and limits on the number of guns one person can buy in a month. They present statistics that compare high numbers of gun-related deaths in the United States with lower numbers in countries with more stringent regulations on gun ownership and usage. The most absolute gun control advocates believe the Second Amendment should be interpreted narrowly, granting the right to bear arms only in the context of military service.

In the fall of 2002, the area around Washington, D.C. was traumatized by a series of murders committed using a sniper rifle. After three weeks of frightening uncertainty, with ten dead

Who Administers Gun Laws?

The responsibility of enforcing all federal gun laws rests with the Secretary of the Treasury. The Bureau of Alcohol, Tobacco, and Firearms (ATF), a subsection of Treasury, oversees most of the laws currently in effect; the exception is the exportation provisions of the Arms Export Control Act (AECA), which is the domain of the State Department and the U.S. Customs Service.

and three wounded, police arrested John Allen Muhammad and John Lee Malvo. These two soon faced multiple murder charges in which some of the strongest evidence against them came from the "ballistic fingerprint" of a gun allegedly found in their car.[1]

The case increased public interest in creating a national electronic database of "ballistic fingerprints" based on test-firing records that gun manufacturers would be required to create for each gun before sale. The U.S. Bureau of Alcohol, Tobacco, and Firearms (ATF) already helps local police investigators with its Integrated Ballistic Identification System (IBIS), which makes automated comparisons that can sometimes find important links between crimes. An ATF report said recently, "Numerous violent crimes involving firearms have been solved through use of the system, many of which would not have been solved without it."[2]

The National Rifle Association opposed the idea, arguing in a position paper that the state of Maryland, which adopted a ballistic fingerprinting law in 2000, had dramatically reduced

THE LETTER OF THE LAW

The Arms Export Control Act (AECA), 22 U.S.C. §2778

The Arms Export Control Act (AECA) gives the president the authority to control imports and exports of "defense articles," including firearms and ammunition, in furtherance of world peace and the security and foreign policy of the United States. The AECA requires permits and licenses to import and export such articles and prohibits imports from and exports to certain "proscribed countries." The Department of the Treasury administers the import controls of the AECA and has delegated this authority to the Bureau of Alcohol, Tobacco, and Firearms. The State Department and the Customs Service administer and enforce the AECA's export controls.

the sale of handguns, and had spent some $3 million in doing so, but had not solved any crimes using its database. It further argued that a gun's "fingerprint" changes with age and use and that criminals can alter the print further by changing a gun's parts.

In New Jersey, however, a ballistic database proposal, Bill A438, was making progress in the state Assembly in the fall of 2002. As of late October, the New Jersey bill called for ballistic fingerprinting for all guns sold in the state and additional voluntary ballistic fingerprinting for guns already in private hands.[3]

Nearly half of U.S. households contain at least one firearm; these guns are most often purchased for sport, hunting, or self-defense. Opponents of gun control believe that it limits law-abiding citizens' access to guns that are valuable for self-defense and recreation—and that they have a constitutionally guaranteed right to own and use. Opponents of control argue that because only law-abiding citizens will obey gun laws, such laws will give the advantage to criminals. They believe that the Second Amendment guarantees an individual right to bear arms, almost unconditionally.

> **If the manufacture and sale of firearms were banned, what would need to be done about the firearms already in existence?**

Despite all the constitutional arguments on both sides, the debate over the control of guns can be seen as cultural—a rift between those who have been raised in a gun culture, to whom the tradition of gun ownership is personally meaningful, and those who have not and are uncomfortable around firearms. To say this, of course, is to oversimplify the argument; subarguments abound concerning, for example, self-defense, government interference in personal liberties, the balance of power between citizens and criminals, and the risk inherent in the very presence of a gun. Whatever the motivations, though, the public debate is based on law and policy—on interpretation of the Second Amendment, on the relationship of gun incidence to crime rates, and on the risk of gun-related injury to the public.

The Second Amendment Guarantees the Right to Bear Arms

The Framers of the Constitution believed that every "man" should be armed.

Early American colonists had many uses for firearms. A good musket could supply a family with food, protect against attacks by wild animals, and serve as a weapon against the preexisting populations who objected, often violently, to the colonial presence. After more than 200 years of British rule, the colonists found a new use for firearms: revolution. The original 13 colonies, with growing economic and cultural sophistication, had become dissatisfied with what they saw as oppressive foreign rule. England's King George III, unlike the increasingly rebellious colonists, believed his nation was the motherland and the distant American colonies were her unruly children. The colonists bristled under the King's relentless demands. They were taxed but did not receive representation in the English

Actor Charlton Heston, who became president of the NRA, proclaims that he will keep his gun until someone pries it from his "cold, dead hands." The anti-control side of the argument can be characterized as a fight for personal liberties; this interpretation sees the Second Amendment's call for a "well-regulated Militia" as a defense against oppressive government that is still relevant, even if in a different form.

government. They were forced to give lodging to English troops and to provide a market for English goods. In 1776, the colonies declared independence and went to war with their rulers.

The American Revolution, which ended in 1783, would not have been a possibility without firearms. Historians believe the superior range of the "Pennsylvania rifle," a product designed and manufactured by German settlers, was responsible for giving the revolutionists an early advantage in battles against British troops.

Time after time, the people who oppose gun control and favor the right to bear arms return to the early American stories of oppression, rebellion, and eventual freedom. The American

Revolution sets the backdrop for the argument for the right to bear arms.

However, the debate really begins with the Second Amendment to the Constitution. The U.S. Constitution created the framework for the nation's legal system; it created the foundation upon which the structure of American society is built. The men who wrote the Constitution, the Framers, engaged in a long debate over the 27 words of the Second Amendment:

> A well-regulated Militia, being necessary to the security of a free State, the right of the people to keep and bear Arms, shall not be infringed.

When the Framers drafted the Constitution, military defense was a necessary consideration. The substance of their debate is of great concern to modern policymakers, for both advocates and opponents of gun control make historical arguments about the meaning of the Second Amendment. Each side uses differences in interpretation to find evidence that the Framers intended to draft an amendment that supports one side over the other.

Does the vague wording of the Second Amendment make the right to bear arms less important than other constitutional rights?

Seen from the historical perspective advocated by gun control opponents, there were two main motivations for the Second Amendment. First, U.S. citizens had inherited from the British system a respect for the rights of citizens to arm themselves. The judge-made English "common law" included a provision protecting the right to bear arms. In a sense, this argument asserts that the right to bear arms was passed down, along with other traditions, from the British motherland to the American colonies.

Second, the revolutionary experience had instilled in the colonists a fundamental distrust of federal governments. A permanent national military, or standing army, epitomized the kind of centralized power that concerned them. A system of state militias was seen as a preventive measure against dependency on the protection of a standing army. In each state, militias of self-armed men were called upon to defend their country themselves. By relying on loosely organized groups of armed citizens, the Framers believed they could protect the young nation from arbitrary and tyrannical rule.

Gun control opponents quote the Framers themselves in defending their interpretation of history. It is important to understand that most of the Framers' references to "men" really mean "able-bodied free white men"—notably not the colonial slave population. Patrick Henry, a Virginian political leader, said at Virginia's ratification convention, "The great object is that every man be armed. Every man who is able may have a gun." Samuel Adams at the Massachusetts convention: "The Constitution shall never be construed to prevent the people of the United States who are peaceable citizens from keeping their own arms." John Adams: "Arms in the hands of citizens may be used at individual discretion, in private self-defense."[1] Thomas Jefferson modeled much of his thought on the work of the noted contemporary Italian philosopher/criminologist Cesare Beccaria, who argued the absurdity of restricting arms in order to prevent crime:

> **Two centuries have passed since the Framers debated these issues. Is arguing about the meaning of their words worthwhile?**

> The laws that forbid the carrying of arms . . . disarm those only who are neither inclined nor determined to commit crimes. Can it be supposed that those who have the courage to violate the most sacred laws of humanity, the most important of the code, will respect the less important and arbitrary ones, which can be violated with impunity, and which, if strictly obeyed, would put an end to personal liberty—so

dear to men, so dear to the enlightened legislator—and subject innocent persons to all the vexations that the guilty alone ought to suffer? Such laws make things worse for the assaulted and better for the assailants; they serve rather to encourage than prevent homicides, for an unarmed man may be attacked with greater confidence than an armed man.[2]

Jefferson copied this passage in its entirety into his personal "commonplace book."

The Federalist Papers—two volumes of essays, printed in 1787 and 1788, that argued in favor of ratifying the Constitution—also contain arguments in favor of arming the citizenry. James Madison, the author of the Second Amendment, noted in the Papers that U.S. citizens had "the advantage of being armed"—a boon lost in other nations, where governments did not trust armed citizens.[3] Alexander Hamilton of New York wrote, "[I]f circumstances should at any time oblige the government to form an army of any magnitude, that army can never be formidable to the liberties of the people while there is a large body of citizens, little if at all inferior to them in discipline and the use of arms, who stand ready to defend their rights and those of their fellow citizens."[4] Another saying of Hamilton's is quoted even more often: "The best we can hope for concerning the people at large is that they be properly armed."[5]

What did the Framers mean?

When gun control advocates argue that the modern National Guard fulfills the duties of the militia of the Second Amendment, opponents counter with arguments that the militias intended by the Framers were grass-roots citizens' organizations. All eligible men were *de facto* members. The National Guard, a system of armed forces run by each of the 50 states established in 1903, is too formal, in the view of gun control opponents, to replace the citizen-run militias. In 1920

Congress deemed the National Guard to be only one part, not the whole, of the "Militia of the United States."

Militias were frequently deployed for community and national defense; they were called upon to quell uprisings and rebellions—among slaves, native populations, or other Europeans—as well as to defend the nation during the War of 1812 and the Civil War. One year after the addition of the Second Amendment, the U.S. Congress passed the Militia Act of 1792, which required all able-bodied free white men to arm themselves and serve as members of local militias. The Act stated, "Every citizen . . . [shall] provide himself with a good musket, or firelock, a sufficient bayonet and belt, [and] two spare flints. . . ." The significance that gun control opponents see in this wording is that it specifies that the militia applied to almost everyone, at least as far as most laws at the time did. Akhil Reed Amar, of the Yale Law School, and Alan Hirsch, a former *Yale Law Journal* editor, wrote:

> We recall that the Framers' militia was not an elite fighting force but the entire citizenry of the time: all able-bodied adult white males. Since the Second Amendment explicitly declares that its purpose is to preserve a well-regulated militia, the right to bear arms was universal in scope. The vision animating the amendment was nothing less than popular sovereignty—applied in the military realm. The Framers recognized that self-government requires the People's access to bullets as well as ballots. The armed citizenry (militia) was expected to protect against not only foreign enemies, but also a potentially tyrannical federal government. In short, the right to bear arms was intended to ensure that our government remained in the hands of the People.[6]

The Framers' "militia" existed at a time when the U.S. Army, Navy, Air Force, Marine Corps, Coast Guard, and National Guard did not exist to protect citizens. Still, these all are government entities. Is the idea of a militia still relevant?

The right to bear arms applies to individuals.

Understanding the idea of a militia as a loose group of individual citizens, and not a formal, government-sponsored military body, is a key to understanding the scope of the debate over the Second Amendment. Gun control opponents believe that the Framers intended the Second Amendment to be interpreted as an individual right, a right granted to each person as a self-sufficient entity. This position draws on the legacy of individual rights in the United States, on the belief that American rights, by definition, belong to the people as individuals, not as a group. Other individual rights protected by the Constitution include the freedom of speech, the freedom of religion, and the right to be protected from unreasonable searches and seizures. Gun control advocates, conversely, believe that the Second Amendment applies only to the people as a group, meaning the people who collectively form the militia.

The Second Amendment is contained in the Bill of Rights, the first ten amendments to the Constitution. Gun control opponents believe that the Bill of Rights as a whole was meant to protect *individual* liberties. To bolster the historical basis of their position, gun control opponents return to the words of the Framers: Madison, for example, wrote that the Bill of Rights was "calculated to secure the personal rights of the people." Albert Gallatin, the Secretary of the Treasury under Thomas Jefferson, said, "[I]t establishes some rights of the individual as unalienable and which consequently, no majority has a right to deprive them of."[7]

In the Declaration of Independence, the document that announced the colonists' intention to break free from royal rule, Jefferson wrote that "all men are created equal" and "are endowed by their Creator with certain unalienable rights"— that is, rights that cannot be taken away from them by any government. In contrast with the natural rights of the people, he wrote that government derives its powers from the consent of the governed. Gun control opponents rely on an interpretation of the Constitution in which the term "the people" applies to each individual person in the United States, irrespective of that person's membership in a larger organization, such as a militia or a church. This interpretation construes gun ownership as an individual right, one that can be claimed by any person, rather than a collective right. This is among the key points of the debate.

Does the U.S. Constitution grant rights, or protect rights that already exist?

In other words, does it empower a person to do a certain thing, or does it prohibit the government from *stopping* that person from doing that thing?

An interpretation of the rights of the people as the rights of individuals was offered in *United States v. Verdugo-Urquidez* (1990):

> "[T]he people" seems to have been a term of art employed in select parts of the Constitution. The Preamble declares that the Constitution is ordained and established by "the People of the United States." The Second Amendment protects "the right of the people to keep and bear Arms," and the Ninth and Tenth Amendments provide that certain rights and powers are retained by and reserved to "the people."... It suggests that "the people" protected by the Fourth Amendment, and by the First and Second Amendments, and to whom rights and powers are reserved in the Ninth and Tenth Amendments, refers to a class of persons who are a part of a national community or who have otherwise developed sufficient connection with this country to be considered part of that community.[8]

A recent federal appeals decision has weakened pro–gun control arguments based on *United States v. Miller*.

The U.S. Supreme Court has yet to deliver an opinion that definitively supports either side in the debate over gun control and the Second Amendment. The landmark rulings on the subject, in lower courts as well as the high court, have been interpreted favorably by both sides.

The first Supreme Court case to consider federal regulation of firearms in light of the Second Amendment was the leading case of *United States v. Miller* (1939).[9] On April 18, 1938, Frank Miller and James Layton drove from Oklahoma to Arkansas and were charged with unlawfully transporting a firearm—in this case, an unregistered sawed-off shotgun—over state lines without a permit, in violation of the National Firearms Act of 1934. (Jack Miller was a member of the Irish O'Malley gang and had participated in several bank robberies. When four men against whom he had testified broke out of prison, Miller began to fear for his life. Historians have speculated that this fear drove Miller to keep a weapon by his side during all his travels.) After their arrest and indictment, in 1938, they were apprehended and charged with violating the Act, which prohibited the unlicensed transportation of short-barreled guns. In their defense, Miller and Layton pleaded that the law violated the Second Amendment. The government appealed a district court ruling that had been granted in the defendants' favor.

In a ruling issued in 1939, the Supreme Court held that the "obvious purpose" of the Second Amendment was "to assure the continuation and render possible the effectiveness" of state militias. The Court added, "It must be interpreted and applied with that end in view."

THE LETTER OF THE LAW

The National Firearms Act of 1934

The National Firearms Act (NFA) regulates certain classes of firearms, such as machine-guns, short-barrel rifles, short-barrel shotguns, silencers, and destructive devices. The NFA requires that these weapons be registered by their makers, manufacturers, and importers and imposes taxes on transactions involving such weapons.

Gun control opponents found some support for their arguments in the decision. Gun control advocates believe the Court's opinion requires a connection to military service for the bearing of arms to be protected. Gun control opponents believe the opposite: that a connection to military service must be disproved before the right to bear arms can be limited. Pointing to historical evidence that Revolutionary War–era militias required their members to bring their own arms, they argue that the Second Amendment was meant to make it possible for citizens to buy and keep their own weapons. In their narrow interpretation of the *Miller* ruling, gun control opponents believe the Court approved the restriction of the right to bear arms only if the weapon had no connection to military or militia use—a hard case to make if, as they believe, almost every gun could be used for militia service.

In *United States v. Emerson,*[10] a case regarding a man found guilty of possessing a firearm while under a restraining order for domestic violence, the Court of Appeals for the Fifth Circuit upheld the conviction but agreed with gun control opponents that the Second Amendment applies to people individually.

The appeals court's 2001 opinion rejected the pro–gun control interpretation of *Miller,* which viewed the right to bear arms as a collectively held right intended solely for the maintenance of the militia. The *Emerson* opinion stated that the Second Amendment, like the rest of the Bill of Rights, was written with the intention of protecting that right for all citizens, whether they belong to a militia or not.

The court ruled that restrictions on gun ownership must be "limited, narrowly tailored specific exceptions or restrictions for particular cases that are reasonable and not inconsistent with the right of U.S. citizens generally to individually keep and bear their private arms as historically understood in this country." Restrictions on gun ownership by "felons, infants, and those of unsound mind," the court ruled, were constitutional.

Although widely lauded as a victory by gun control opponents, the Fifth Circuit court's opinion does not extend to the rest of the country. Nor does it overturn the Supreme Court's *Miller* decision—it only interprets it narrowly. The arguments it sets forth may *influence* other jurisdictions, but they by no means change national precedent.

FROM THE BENCH

From *United States v. Miller*, 307 U.S. 174 (1939)

In the absence of any evidence tending to show that possession or use of a "shotgun having a barrel of less than eighteen inches in length" at this time has some reasonable relationship to the preservation or efficiency of a well regulated militia, we cannot say that the Second Amendment guarantees the right to keep and bear such an instrument. Certainly it is not within judicial notice that this weapon is any part of the ordinary military equipment or that its use could contribute to the common defense....

The Constitution as originally adopted granted to the Congress power "To provide for calling forth the Militia to execute the Laws of the Union, suppress Insurrections and repel Invasions; To provide for organizing, arming, and disciplining, the Militia, and for governing such Part of them as may be employed in the Service of the United States, reserving to the States respectively, the Appointment of the Officers, and the Authority of training the Militia according to the discipline prescribed by Congress." With obvious purpose to assure the continuation and render possible the effectiveness of such forces the declaration and guarantee of the Second Amendment were made. It must be interpreted and applied with that end in view.

The Militia which the States were expected to maintain and train is set in contrast with Troops which they were forbidden to keep without the consent of Congress. The sentiment of the time strongly disfavored standing armies; the common view was that adequate defense of country and laws could be secured through the Militia—civilians primarily, soldiers on occasion.

The signification attributed to the term *Militia* appears from the debates in the Convention, the history and legislation of Colonies and States, and the writings of approved commentators. These show plainly enough that the Militia comprised all males physically capable of acting in concert for the common defense. "A body of citizens enrolled for military discipline." And further, that ordinarily when called for service these men were expected to appear bearing arms supplied by themselves and of the kind in common use at the time.

The right to bear arms is fundamental to liberty.
Gun control opponents view the right to bear arms as an individual liberty. In the same vein, they think that efforts to limit access to guns are tantamount to repression. Furthermore, they believe the liberties that made the United States into the strong nation that it is today encompass the right to bear arms. Charlton Heston, an actor who became president of the NRA in 1998, spoke at Harvard Law

FROM THE BENCH

United States v. Emerson, 270 F.3d 203 (5th Cir. 2001)

Dr. Timothy Joe Emerson, embroiled in a divorce with his estranged wife, was enjoined by restraining order from coming near her or her daughter. Under the Violence Against Women Act (1994), the restraining order prohibited Emerson from owning a gun. After he allegedly threatened his wife and her child with a Beretta pistol, Emerson was indicted and charged with a weapons violation. Emerson's collection of firearms included an M-1 carbine, an SKS assault rifle with a bayonet, and an M-14 assault rifle. The NRA argued that the charges violated Emerson's Second Amendment rights. In 1999, the U.S. District Court for the Northern District of Texas agreed. Judge Samuel Cummings dismissed the indictment and ruled that the federal law barring people under restraining orders from owning guns was an unconstitutional violation of the Second Amendment. In 2001, The U.S. Court of Appeals for the Fifth Circuit overturned the trial court's ruling, stating that the law in question did *not* violate the Constitution. The case was remanded to the district court, which charged Emerson again with illegal possession of a firearm.

Despite the reversal of the lower court's ruling, gun control opponents view the decision as a victory. In a written opinion that is classified as *dictum*—a nonbinding opinion that does not concern the material facts of the case—the court argued for an individual rights interpretation of the Second Amendment. It described a limited take on this interpretation, arguing that the right to bear arms belongs to individual citizens but is subject to certain limitations.

In 2002, the Supreme Court declined without comment to hear *United States v. Emerson*. The Court's decision has been interpreted as a tacit acceptance of the Fifth Circuit court's finding that the Second Amendment protects an individual right.

School in 1999 about his passionate view on gun control: "I believe that we are again engaged in a great civil war, a cultural war that's about to hijack your birthright to think and say what resides in your heart. I fear you no longer trust the pulsing lifeblood of liberty inside you ... the stuff that made this country rise from wilderness into the miracle that it is."

Is gun ownership contingent on membership in a larger group?

Would mandatory membership in a group like the NRA be an effective way to regulate gun ownership?

The Second Amendment is permanently connected to colonial times and the United States' efforts to rise above foreign rule. These links to great struggles imbue the right to bear arms with feelings of power and strength, qualities that are part of the nation's psyche. Neal Knox, a libertarian member of the NRA who helped to guide the organization toward a more staunchly anti–gun control position in the 1970s, has said that "gun control is about power; the person with the guns has the power."

Gun rights activists see the right to bear arms as emblematic of a larger conservative effort to keep the government out of private lives. The less control the government has over individual behavior, conservatives believe, the better. In the same vein, they argue against bans on public smoking and environmental restrictions on manufacturers whose products may be harmful to the ecology or to humans.

How much control should the government have over the lives of its citizens?

What are the advantages and disadvantages of such control?

Although opponents of gun control tend to be politically on the right, some extreme leftists—notably the African-American separatist Black Panther Party—have also advocated using guns in self-defense against the government in times of repression.

This belief is also part of a more traditional interpretation of the Second Amendment, which argues that the Framers of the Constitution wanted to ensure that U.S. citizens had the ability to overthrow tyrannical or oppressive rulers.

———————•———————•———————•———————

From a gun rights point of view, the right to keep and bear arms is a guarantee of American freedom. The prevalent pro-gun view associates individual firearm ownership with the memory that, at the time of the Constitution's framing, the newly independent citizens rejected a professional standing army in favor of an informal citizens' militia. The Supreme Court in *United States v. Miller* found that the Second Amendment did not bar Congress from prohibiting the transportation of sawed-off shotguns, but the Court has otherwise spoken only rarely on the issue of gun control. A recent federal appeals court decision interpreted *Miller* narrowly, reinforcing the contention of pro-gun advocates that gun ownership rights belong to citizens as individuals, not to citizens as members of an official "militia" or other national defense force. Although there have been some left-wing opponents of gun control, most pro-gun advocacy is closely associated with a conservative individualism that also opposes other kinds of government interference in people's personal lives.

Gun Activists Misconstrue the Second Amendment

The NRA and anti–gun control groups use the Second Amendment to anchor their position that gun ownership in the United States should be unrestricted or only minimally restricted. Critics say these activists latch on to the superficial meaning of the Second Amendment without acknowledging the limits on gun ownership set forward by the very people who drafted the Constitution. Former Supreme Court Chief Justice Warren Burger voiced this position powerfully in 1991:

> [The Second Amendment] is the subject of one of the greatest pieces of fraud, I repeat the word *fraud*, on the American public by special interest groups that I have ever seen in my lifetime. . . . [Opponents of gun control have] misled the American people and they, I regret to say, they have had far too much influence on the Congress of the United States than as a citizen I would like to see—and I am a gun man.[1]

In Burger's view, the Second Amendment cannot be viewed as permitting citizens to own arms without restriction and to argue otherwise is to misrepresent the Amendment's language.

The "right to bear arms" depends on the need for a militia.

Gun control advocates believe that the Second Amendment, unlike other amendments, cannot be separated from its stated purpose, the need for a militia. The First Amendment specifically enumerates the rights of speech, religion, and the press: "Congress shall make no law respecting an establishment of religion, or prohibiting the free exercise thereof; or abridging the freedom of speech, or of the press. . . ." These rights are plainly stated, with no exceptions specified.

> **Is the importance of guns to early Americans relevant to gun control issues today?**
>
> **Can private gun ownership help repel a foreign invasion?**

The Second Amendment, on the other hand, begins with a preamble that states the purpose for the right: "a well-regulated militia." By stating that purpose first, gun control advocates believe, the Framers intended to set boundaries on the right. They interpret the preamble's "A well regulated Militia, being necessary to the security of a free State" to mean "For the sole reason that a militia is needed to protect a free nation."

James Madison, who penned the Second Amendment, made the defense-related goal of his law apparent in his original draft: "The right of the people to keep and bear arms shall not be infringed; a well armed and well regulated militia being the best security of a free country; but no person religiously scrupulous of bearing arms shall be compelled to render military service in person." The last clause addressed those with religious objections to military service and exempted them from duty. Although the Senate ultimately dropped the religious exemption clause, Madison's use of it establishes his understanding that to "bear Arms" was to provide military service, not to simply own guns.

There is no longer a need for a militia, so there is no longer a right to bear arms.

In the late 20th century, self-organized groups of civilian citizens calling themselves *militias* began cropping up in rural and suburban communities. These loosely organized groups have little in common with a "well-regulated militia." Unlike today's "citizen militias," composed of antigovernment extremists, the militias of the early United States were by definition compulsory and dedicated to protecting the nation. At the time of the signing of the Constitution, 1787, virtually all able-bodied white men in the fledgling states were required to report for service in state militias. These state-run forces performed the duties of a standing army in a country that was fearful of concentrating too much power with the central government.

Do citizens need guns as protection against their government?

Without a militia, what protects against a violent overthrow of the U.S. government?

When the National Guard was created in 1903, the necessity for a militia was, according to gun control advocates, eliminated. Thus, they argue, the need for citizens to arm themselves diminished.

The Second Amendment protects gun ownership as a collective right, not as an individual right.

Why is it important to differentiate between individual rights and group rights?

Which are more important?

The interpretation of the Second Amendment championed by gun control advocates centers on the degree to which the militia-based need, in the aftermath of the Revolution, for the right to bear arms limits the rights of citizens to arm themselves today. Gun control advocates conclude that the Framers' original purpose gives the government great latitude in restricting public gun possession in the name of public safety. Until 2001, the U.S. circuit courts endorsed the "militia" interpretation of the Second Amendment. But in 2001, *United States v. Emerson*, a decision much more favorable to gun owners, emerged from the Fifth Circuit Court of Appeals—that is, the federal appeals court for Texas, Louisiana, and Mississippi.

Breaking ranks with the other circuit courts, the Fifth Circuit panel embraced the individual-rights interpretation of the Second Amendment. The opinion, which is not binding on

FROM THE BENCH

From *United States v. Emerson*, 270 F.3d 203 (5th Cir. 2001)

We reject the collective rights and sophisticated collective rights models for interpreting the Second Amendment. We hold, consistent with *Miller,* that it protects the right of individuals, including those not then actually a member of any militia or engaged in active military service or training, to privately possess and bear their own firearms, such as the pistol involved here, that are suitable as personal, individual weapons and are not of the general kind or type excluded by *Miller.* ...

The district court held that section 922(g)(8) [of the U.S. code] was unconstitutionally overbroad because it allows Second Amendment rights to be infringed absent any express judicial finding that the person subject to the order posed a future danger. In other words, the section 922(g)(8) threshold for deprivation of the fundamental right to keep and bear arms [when under a restraining order] is too low.

Although, as we have held, the Second Amendment *does* protect individual rights, that does not mean that those rights may never be made subject to any limited, narrowly tailored specific exceptions or restrictions for particular cases that are reasonable and not inconsistent with the right of U.S. citizens generally to individually keep and bear their private arms as historically understood in this country. ... [I]t is clear that felons, infants and those of unsound mind may be prohibited from possessing firearms. ... In essence, Emerson, and the district court, concede that had the order contained an express finding, on the basis of adequate evidence, that Emerson actually posed a credible threat to the physical safety of his wife, and had that been a genuinely contested matter at the hearing ... then Emerson could, consistent with the Second Amendment, be precluded from possessing a firearm while he remained subject to the order.

jurisdictions outside the Fifth Circuit states, was read as a sign that courts might begin to narrow their interpretation of the 1939 *Miller* ruling, which embraced a collective-rights view of the Second Amendment. *Emerson* suggested that, as an individual right, the right to bear arms may be protected even when the arms in question have little connection to military service.

Gun control advocates were outraged. "The Fifth Circuit's ruling in . . . *Emerson* achieves the right result for the wrong reasons," said Dennis Henigan, director of the Legal Action Project of the Brady Center to Prevent Gun Violence. "We are pleased that the court rejected the National Rifle Association's extremist view that would have guaranteed Timothy Joe Emerson the right to own an arsenal, even though he was the subject of a domestic violence restraining order and had threatened his wife with a handgun. But the court's suggestion that the Second Amendment guarantees an individual right to be armed for reasons unrelated to organized militia service is based on a gross distortion of U.S. constitutional history and the prior rulings of the U.S. Supreme Court. It is obvious that two judges of the Fifth Circuit sought to use this case to propound their theory of the Second Amendment, but it is a theory that has been soundly rejected by every other federal appeals court."[2]

In June of 2002 the Supreme Court declined, without comment, to hear appeals both of *Emerson* and of another case, *Haney v. United States*, in which the Tenth Circuit upheld a federal law banning private ownership of machine guns. The U.S. Department of Justice (DOJ), which under Attorney General John Ashcroft began to express strong support for gun owners' rights, had asked the Supreme Court not to review either case. The Department of Justice briefs that opposed review of *Haney* and *Emerson* both expressed support for *Emerson*'s interpretation of the Second Amendment as protecting an individual right to bear arms while allowing "limited,

Did the court reach the right conclusion in *Emerson*?

narrowly tailored specific exceptions or restrictions" like the anti–domestic violence law involved in *Emerson*. Additionally, attached to both briefs was a letter from Ashcroft that endorsed the *Emerson* case but also said, "The Department can and will continue to defend vigorously the constitutionality, under the Second Amendment, of all existing federal firearms laws."

Henigan wrote in response to the denial of review, "The action of the United States Supreme Court today in denying review of the lower court rulings in *Haney v. United States* and *Emerson v. United States* provides no comfort to the extremist gun lobby and others who view the Second Amendment as a weapon against reasonable gun laws. It remains true that never in our nation's history has a federal court struck down a gun law on Second Amendment grounds."[3]

> **The court ruled against Emerson, so what difference does it make what the judges think about the Second Amendment?**

"The right to bear arms" is not an absolute right.

The freedoms set forth in the Bill of Rights, gun control advocates argue, have never been absolute—that is, there are exceptions to them. As Oliver Wendell Holmes famously declared in *Schenck v. United States* (1919),[4] the freedom of speech does not protect people who mischievously yell "fire" in a crowded theater—for the government has an interest in protecting its citizens and so must weigh the public interest against that individual right. Nor does the freedom of speech protect newspapers that knowingly publish false information from being sued by the affected parties. Likewise, for most moderate policymakers, the debate is not about *whether* the Constitution allows for gun control; it is about the *extent* to which the state and federal governments should regulate ownership and use. Most U.S. citizens seem to favor some kind of gun control; CNN and Harris polls conducted in the spring of 2000 both found that about 60 percent of Americans supported stricter gun laws.[5]

A major target of gun control legislation is the Saturday Night Special—any small, inexpensive handgun. These guns are frequently used in crimes, so banning them seems logical; but anti–gun control groups argue that to restrict access to these is to deny self-protection to people who cannot afford more expensive firearms.

Centrist groups, such as the Brady Center to Prevent Gun Violence (named in honor of wounded Presidential aide Jim Brady), believe that hunters and those who use firearms for legitimate sport should be allowed to continue their hobbies. Hunting is a true pastime in the United States and contributes to the happiness of millions of citizens. The careful regulation or outright banning of handguns and assault weapons would, the Brady organization and others argue, keep guns designed to kill *people* out of circulation, allowing hunters to preserve their pastime.

Others take a more radical approach. Some gun control advocates say the Second Amendment has become an anachronism, a relic that is no longer applicable in modern life. Semiautomatic handguns and assault rifles did not exist during the Revolution and have caused problems that the Framers could never have envisioned. These gun control advocates lobby for outright banning of all guns.

Staunch gun rights activists argue the other extreme: that the Second Amendment provides an incontrovertible privilege to own guns to all U.S. citizens, even those, like Timothy Joe Emerson, who pose a threat to others. Often, the NRA argues that this right is based on the possibility of tyranny. If our government became undemocratic and repressive, they argue, citizens would need to protect themselves.

Gun control advocates say this logic leads straight to a very dangerous result: citizens armed with even more dangerous weapons such as nuclear arms, rocket launchers, and missiles. If one accepts that the Second Amendment provides a blanket protection of the right to bear arms, of any type, by anyone, and if this right is aimed at allowing citizens to rise up against their own government, then it follows that ordinary people should have easy access to military weapons. U.S. citizens would need bazookas and tanks, grenade launchers, and nuclear weapons to fight the full force of the country's military. In addition to the obvious impracticality of this situation, control advocates say, the Constitution actually prohibits citizens from going to war against their government. The crime of treason is spelled out in Article III, Section 3: "Treason against the United States shall consist only in levying war against them, or in adhering to their enemies, giving them aid and comfort." Gun control advocates say that an unlimited right to bear arms would be tantamount to including a suicide clause in the Constitution.

> **Are other liberties threatened if the right to bear arms is threatened?**

Justice Burger said: "The very language of the Second Amendment refutes any argument that it was intended to guarantee every citizen an unfettered right to any kind of weapon. . . . [S]urely the Second Amendment does not remotely guarantee every person the constitutional right to have a 'Saturday Night Special' or a machine gun without any regulation whatever.

There is no support in the Constitution for the argument that federal and state governments are powerless to regulate the purchase of such firearms. . . ."[1]

The American "gun heritage" is largely mythical.

Gun control opponents often sell their case by relying on the symbolic power of the United States' history of gun use. However, the image of the gun-toting colonist has been called into question by historians and gun control advocates in recent years. Michael Bellesiles, a history professor at Emory University, published findings in 1999 that suggested that few U.S. citizens owned guns in the nation's early years. According to his survey of estate wills, fewer than 10 percent of citizens owned firearms until 1850.[6] Today, at least 40 percent of U.S. households contain guns. Hollywood "Westerns" portray frontier towns as wild outposts where the sheriffs were no match for sharp-shooting bandits. Most Western towns, however, had strict laws restricting gun ownership within city limits. Samuel Colt, the gun manufacturer credited with encouraging the image of the gun-slinging American man, also coined a slogan that encompasses the mythological passion of the nation's love affair with the gun: "God may have made men, but Sam Colt made them equal." It says something about the true role of guns in U.S. history that Colt's brother, John, was tried in 1841 for murdering his creditor—with a hammer.[7]

What is the prevailing image of pro-gun lobbyists?

How do the pro-control and the anti-control groups see one another?

How extensive is the role of stereotypes—of gun owners, of early Americans, of anti-gun activists, of criminals— in the debate over gun control?

Bellesiles became the subject of an extensive lobbying campaign by pro-gun advocates, including the NRA and columnists in conservative journals. He received death threats, and his supporters and employers received angry letters.

On a more scholarly level, some academics challenged the accuracy of his reports on early American probate records and questioned whether public records really would have existed for all the guns actually available to early Americans. Along with specific answers to critics, Bellesiles has stated that important research notes for the book were destroyed by a flood at his office. The book won the prestigious Bancroft Prize, and Bellesiles received statements of support from the American Historical Association and other reputable scholarly organizations. On the other hand, Emory University took the critics' charges of sloppiness and even falsification seriously enough to investigate. The Emory investigating committee's report supported several of the charges. In October of 2002, Bellesiles announced he would resign his professorship, citing a "hostile environment."[8]

———————————————

The most adamant supporters of gun control argue that the Second Amendment refers to the use of weapons in the national defense, and does not confer an individual right to bear arms. Meanwhile, some centrist gun control advocates want to preserve hunting and sport uses of guns within limits. The centrist Brady Center argues that the Fifth Circuit's 2001 *Emerson* decision is an aberrant decision not paralleled in the other federal circuit courts. Gun control advocates generally see the pro-gun rhetoric about physically fighting a tyrannical government as both impractical and alarming and note that it essentially legitimizes the crime of treason. There is also the question of whether guns were as important in the days of the Founding Fathers as gun advocates would have us believe; Professor Michael Bellesiles has argued otherwise and has been the subject of an intense campaign to discredit his views.

Gun Control Laws Reduce Violence

The gun-related death rate in the United States is higher than that of any other industrialized nation. More than 25,000 U.S. citizens die every year from gunshot wounds. Young people are especially at risk: in 1998, 10 children and teenagers were killed every day by firearms, and firearms are the second most frequent cause of death *overall* for U.S. citizens ages 15 to 24.[1] Gun control advocates predict that gunfire may soon surpass cars as the leading cause of unnatural death among children. Franklin Zimring and Gordon Hawkins cite the use of firearms in assault and robbery as "the single environmental feature of American society that is most clearly linked to the extraordinary death rate from interpersonal violence in the United States." These researchers conclude that, "without

Would enacting strict gun laws reduce the number of guns in the hands of criminals?

strategies for the reduction of firearm use in assaults, no policy can be accurately characterized as directed at the reduction of American lethal violence."[2]

The high rates of gun-related death in the U.S. are a result of permissive gun control.

U.S. gun laws generally make it easy for adults to purchase firearms. Existing restrictions ban certain groups from purchasing guns—children, people with diminished mental capacity, and criminals—and require background checks and waiting periods on licensed sales. However, many sales proceed with no background check on the buyer, and few records of who buys guns are kept. Some cities and states, such as Chicago and Washington, D.C., place higher restrictions on gun sales and some even ban certain types of guns altogether.

One basic truth leads the argument for gun control: guns are deadlier than any other weapon. An assault with a firearm is five times more likely to lead to death than is an assault involving a knife. Furthermore, approximately 40 percent of U.S. households own firearms. Because of this combination of lethality and prevalence, guns are responsible for most murders in the United States. In 1997, gun-related deaths accounted for 70 percent of all homicides.

The United States has historically had the highest rates of murder and other violent crime of all the industrialized nations. The United States is, among large, industrialized democracies, the only nation in which firearms are the cause of the majority of homicides. The government has collected statistics on homicide and other violent crimes in the United States in the 20th century. Historians believe the U.S. murder rate peaked in 1933 at about 10 murders per every 100,000 citizens per year. The following years marked the beginning of a steady decline in the murder rate, which fell until the mid-1940s, rose slightly at the end of World War II, and continued to decline until 1958, when the rate hit 4.5 murders per 100,000 citizens. In the mid-1960s, the

Aggravated Assault, Types of Weapons Used
Percent Distribution by Region, 2001

Region	Total all weapons	Firearms	Knives or cutting instruments	Other weapons (clubs, blunt objects, etc.)	Personal weapons
Total	100.0	18.3	17.8	36.0	27.9
Northeastern States	100.0	13.9	18.4	33.7	34.0
Midwestern States	100.0	19.4	17.2	35.3	28.1
Southern States	100.0	20.0	19.5	38.7	21.9
Western States	100.0	16.8	15.2	32.7	35.3

homicides increased rapidly, hitting rates of 9 per 100,000, and they didn't plateau until the late 1970s. After falling in the early 1980s, the murder rate made a steep assent during the crack cocaine boom of the late 1980s and early 1990s. In 1991, the murder rate hit 10 per 100,000. A much-heralded decline in violent crime, including murder, began in 1994. However, the trend appears to be reversing itself.[3] While violent crime by itself continues to decline, the FBI reports that its "Crime Index" category of violent crimes and serious property crimes — "murder, forcible rape, robbery, aggravated assault, burglary, larceny-theft, and motor vehicle theft" — did increase in 2001 by 2.1 percent when measured in absolute numbers, and by 0.9 percent when measured as a rate per 100,000 inhabitants.[4]

Although the fluctuations of the murder rate have confounded police and policymakers, they help gun control advocates refute the argument that increased gun ownership reduces crime. During periods of nationally rising crime rates, though, criminologist John Lott conducted research that he believes shows that increased access to concealed weapons could reduce certain kinds of crime.[5]

But gun control advocates say that Lott's research does not hold up during periods of nationally *falling* crime rates. The anti-gun Violence Policy Center (VPC) also claimed when Lott's study came out that the source funding for Lott's University of Chicago fellowship, the John M. Olin Foundation, had continuing close links to its founder's company, the Olin Corporation. The Olin Corporation owns Winchester Ammunition, which the VPC identifies as the largest U.S. producer of ammunition. Lott replied that the charge of association was false, and he persuaded the Associated Press to issue, in his words, "a partial correction stating that the Olin Foundation and Olin Corporation are separate organizations."[6]

> **What factors other than gun ownership contribute to the high crime rates in the United States?**
>
> **Are these rates lower now than they would be with stricter control?**
>
> **Or are they higher?**

A 1999 Brady Center study of Federal Bureau of Investigation (FBI) statistics from 1992 to 1998 also refuted Lott: In states that make it hard for citizens to carry concealed weapons, the violent crime rate fell by an average of 30 percent. In states that allow easy access to concealed weapons, the violent crime rates dropped by much less, just 15 percent. Nationally, violent crime fell by 25 percent.[7]

International comparisons show the benefits of gun control.

Ever since the debate over gun control ignited during the 1960s, advocates have pointed to low firearm-related murder rates in countries such as Japan and England, which have strong gun control policies. In Denmark, where guns are restricted to use for hunting, the homicide rate is one fifth as high as in Ohio, even though the two regions share similar rates of injury from assault. The majority of U.S. homicides are committed with firearms; three fourths of those involve handguns, and there are an estimated 65 million handguns in the United States. The relationship between handgun ownership and high crime can be seen in comparisons to countries that minimize access to handguns. According to data from the National Center for Health Statistics, the U.S. firearms death rate in 1995 was 13.7 per 100,000; in Canada, 3.9 per 100,000; in Australia, 2.9 per 100,000; and in England and Wales, 0.4 per 100,000.

Advocates have been criticized for using studies that compare different countries without considering cultural differences other than attitudes toward gun control that could account for the differences in homicide rates. A novel study released in the 1980s sought to rectify this problem by comparing individual cities that shared many characteristics save one: gun control. The study compared Seattle, Washington, and Vancouver, in the Canadian province of British Columbia. The cities bear remarkable similarities in terms of cultural resources, diversity, and climate. However, they were very different in one respect: Seattle had few gun controls, and Vancouver had many. A comparison of robberies, burglaries, assaults, and homicides in both cities from 1980 through 1986 showed that although assault rates were

Are cross-cultural comparisons reliable?

International Comparisons

Data published by Krug and colleagues in 1998 indicated the following rates for gun deaths per 100,000 population:

USA	14.24
Switzerland	5.31
Scotland	0.54
England & Wales	0.41
Japan	0.05

Data from E.G. Krug, et al., "Firearm-Related Deaths in the United States and 35 Other High- and Upper-Middle-Income Countries," *International Journal of Epidemiology* 27:2(April 1998):214.

only slightly higher in Seattle than in Vancouver, the rate of assault involving firearms was seven times higher in Seattle. The risk of death from homicide was far higher in Seattle than in Vancouver. The additional risk was explained by a nearly 500 percent higher chance of being murdered with a handgun in Seattle. Rates of homicide involving weapons other than guns were not substantially different in the two cities. The study concluded that gun control can reduce homicide significantly.[8]

Tougher enforcement of existing laws won't work.

Gun rights groups have repeatedly argued that existing U.S. gun laws are ignored and that part of the solution to gun violence is stricter enforcement of existing laws. They urge the imposition of harsher penalties for violent crimes and crimes committed with firearms. Acknowledging that some laws could be better enforced, gun control advocates reply that (1) all punishments address criminals only once they've committed crimes and (2) penalties and stiff sentences do nothing to keep guns off the streets in the first place.

> **Would stricter enforcement and tougher sentencing reduce crime?**
>
> **How could law enforcement agencies do a better job of enforcing current regulations?**

The initiatives proposed by advocates of gun control fall into three main categories: limiting access, tracking ownership, and banning some or all firearms.

Through background checks on buyers in all sales and transfers of firearms, dangerous weapons will be kept out of dangerous hands. Since the passage of the Brady Act in 1993, hundreds of thousands of felons and other ineligible buyers have been blocked from purchasing guns. The Brady Act—or, formally, the Brady Handgun Violence Prevention Act[9]— requires an instant background check on all purchases from licensed gun dealers. Sales through unlicensed dealers, though, such as in friendly transfers and at gun shows, do not require a background check. This so-called secondary market accounts for as much as 40 percent of U.S. firearm sales. Gun control advocates say convicted killers are finding these cracks in the system and walking away armed.

Gun control advocates have struggled to respond to arguments that gun laws won't affect secondary or illegal gun markets. Their standard reply is that gun laws will reduce the availability of guns in general, thus limiting the number of arms that trickle into the black market. Critics say these advocates need to better address the question of how to enforce gun control in environments controlled by people who make their living by breaking the law.

The success of the Brady Act illustrates the benefits of legislation.

James S. Brady served as President Ronald Reagan's Press Secretary beginning in January of 1981. His career was interrupted just months later, on March 30, 1981. John Hinckley, a mentally disturbed 25-year-old, then emerged from a crowd and fired at the President with a .22-caliber revolver he'd purchased five months earlier for $29 at Rocky's Pawn Shop in Dallas, Texas. President Reagan, Brady, and two law enforcement officers were

The Brady Act

The Gun Control Act was amended in 1993 by the Brady Act, which provided for, on an interim basis, a five-day waiting period on handgun sales by licensed dealers and manufacturers [18 U.S.C. 922(s)]. The waiting period is designed to give state and local law enforcement officials a chance to perform a criminal records check on the purchaser before the gun is sold. The five-day waiting period provisions of the Brady Act expired in November of 1998 and were replaced with a national instant-check system for all firearms sales [18 U.S.C. 922(t)].

During a 1981 attempt on President Ronald Reagan's life, his Press Secretary James Brady was seriously injured and later devoted his career to gun control. The Brady Center to Prevent Gun Violence is now among the leading voices of the pro-control side of the debate.

hit. Brady was seriously injured with a gunshot wound to the head and became dependent on a wheelchair. The incident inspired Brady and his wife, Sarah, to become involved in the gun control movement. Working with the pro-control group Handgun Control, Inc., now the Brady Center to Prevent Gun Violence, the couple began lobbying for legislation that would require longer background checks on all people who want to purchase firearms. Sarah Brady was named chair of the Center in 1991.

Progress was slow. Finally, on November 30, 1993, President William J. Clinton signed "the Brady Bill" into law. The law took effect on February 28, 1994. It required a five-day waiting period and background check on all handgun purchases through licensed dealers. Today the background check is conducted as part of all retail gun purchases. At the time the law passed,

32 states had no system for background checks. In these states, felons could be cleared to purchase a firearm simply by signing a statement swearing that they had never been convicted of a felony. Although store owners kept these paper forms on file, the statements were rarely revisited or double-checked. Gun control advocates call this the "lie and buy" loophole: one just lies about one's past and buys a gun.

Gun control groups have presented research in recent years that they claim shows an immediate impact from the Brady Act on gun trafficking and gun violence. An analysis of FBI crime statistics released by the Brady Center presents evidence that the Brady Act has led to a reduction in the use of firearms in robberies and assaults, possibly preventing thousands of deaths.[10] The study concluded that during the four years after the law passed, between 1994 and 1998, an estimated 9,368 fewer people died than expected because the percentage of robberies and assaults committed with firearms was declining. The number of aggravated assaults committed with a firearm has since fallen by 31.4 percent. The number of robberies committed with a firearm since 1994 has fallen by 33.7 percent. In addition, the number of all murders fell 23.4 percent, whereas the number of murders committed with a firearm fell 29 percent.

Bans on assault weapons help to control guns that are inappropriate for civilian use.

The Brady Center began as Handgun Control, Inc., a group focused on limiting access to handguns, the weapons responsible for James Brady's injury in 1981 and for the deaths of thousands of U.S. citizens every year. However, before the passage of the Brady Act, a new tragedy refocused the United States' attention on a threat from a different kind of firearm: the assault weapon.

In January of 1989, Patrick Purdy, a mentally disturbed drifter, opened fire on children in a Stockton, California, elementary school playground. He killed 5 children and injured 29. Purdy was armed with a Chinese-made semiautomatic rifle, a

7.62-mm AKM-56S with a detachable 30-round magazine. Although the gun had been legally imported, it bore a remarkable resemblance to banned Chinese and Soviet AK-47 assault rifles. The massacre touched off a flurry of support for new laws that would ban or restrict ownership of so-called assault weapons,

Explanations of Some "Assault Weapon" Characteristics

The Brady Center cites the following features as characteristic of assault weapons:

- *A large-capacity ammunition magazine,* which enables the shooter to continuously fire dozens of rounds without reloading. Standard hunting rifles are usually equipped with no more than three- or four-shot magazines.

- *A folding stock* on a rifle or shotgun, which makes guns easier to conceal.

- *A pistol grip* on a rifle or shotgun, which facilitates firing from the hip, allowing the shooter to spray-fire the weapon. A pistol grip also helps the shooter stabilize the firearm during rapid fire or when firing from the ground and makes it easier to shoot assault rifles one-handed.

- *A barrel shroud,* which is designed to cool the barrel so that the firearm can shoot many rounds in rapid succession without overheating. It also allows the shooter to grasp the barrel area to stabilize the weapon, without incurring serious burns, during rapid fire.

- *A (threaded) barrel* designed to accommodate one of the following:

    (1) *a flash suppressor,* which makes firearms less visible at night and provides stability during rapid fire, helping the shooter maintain control of the firearm;

    (2) *a silencer,* which muffles the sound of gunfire and is rarely used outside of crime; or

    (3) *a bayonet.*

Modified from the Brady Campaign: Facts & Information: Gun Laws. Available online at *www.bradycampaign.org/facts/gunlaws/awb.asp.*

semiautomatic firearms with little sporting or hunting utility that are modeled after military weapons designed to fire large numbers of bullets in just a few seconds. Assault weapons did not exist during the drafting of the Constitution. Because the Framers hardly anticipated the introduction of weapons of such power and lethality, advocates say that assault weapons should be available only for the national defense.

What are the legitimate uses of an assault weapon?

New legislation passed first in California, but the bill was widely regarded as a "quick fix" without the substance to force real change. National attention soon followed, but it wasn't until 1994 that a federal assault weapons ban passed. The federal law was included in the Violent Crime Control and Law Enforcement Act of 1994, which President Clinton signed into law on September 13, 1994. Unless Congress and the President vote to renew the law, the assault weapons ban will expire in 2004. Federal courts have rejected challenges to the law filed by the NRA and other anti-control groups.

Police groups offered broad support for the ban. Although there are no good statistics on the numbers of assault weapons used in crimes, police across the United States in the 1980s reported—and President Clinton picked this up in a 1994 speech at the Ohio Peace Officers Training Academy[11]—that semiautomatic assault weapons had become the "weapon of choice" for drug traffickers, gangs, and paramilitary extremist groups. Before the federal government banned many assault weapons in 1994, the Bureau of Alcohol, Tobacco, and Firearms (ATF) estimated that about 1 percent of about 200 million guns in circulation were assault weapons; this is the most recent data available. In comparison, 8 percent of the gun-tracing requests filed at that time by police involved assault weapons.[12] This suggests that assault weapons are used in crimes more than nonassault weapons.

The assault weapons law banned the production and

Opponents to strong gun control often claim that pro-control arguments are based on fear—of the *appearance* of a gun, rather than on an accurate estimation of its dangerousness. This argument is applied most frequently to assault weapons, but some rifle components, such as hunting scopes, seem to add to the perception. Control opponents reply that education is the key to avoiding accidents and abuse.

importation of certain semiautomatic rifles, pistols and shotguns. It also banned close copies that retained two or more specific elements of the prohibited models. It outlawed magazine cartridges that hold more than 10 rounds of ammunition. Firearms and magazines already in the public's possession were excluded from the ban, as were weapons manufactured for police or military use. The bill bans by name the manufacture of 19 different weapons, including the Israeli UZI, the Intratec TEC-9, and revolving cylinder shotguns such as the ominously named Street Sweeper and Striker 12.

The bill also bans "copies" or "duplicates" of any of the named weapons. Without banning copies, lawmakers would

THE LETTER OF THE LAW

The Assault Weapons Ban

The federal crime bill signed by President Clinton on September 13, 1994, included the Violent Crime Control and Law Enforcement Act of 1994, called the Assault Weapons Ban. This made it a federal crime to possess, sell, or give away an assault weapon. Assault weapons manufactured before the law went into effect were "grandfathered," which means the new ban does apply to those weapons. The law required that assault weapons manufactured after the ban was enacted be stamped with their date of manufacture.

The law defines assault weapons in a variety of ways, affecting more than 175 firearms in all. It takes great care to mention many by name:

> [A]ny of the firearms, or copies or duplicates of the firearms in any caliber, known as: Norinco, Mitchell, Poly Technologies Avtomat Kalashnikovs (all models); Action Arms I.M.I. UZI and Galil; Beretta AR-70 (SC70); Colt AR-15; Fabrique Nationale FN-FAL/LAR, and FNC; SWD M-10, M-11, M-11/9, and M-12; Steyr AUG; Intratec TEC-9, TEC-DC9, and TEC-22; and revolving cylinder shotguns, such as (or similar to) the Street Sweeper and Striker 12....

Other varieties are not named but are described scrupulously:

- A semi-automatic rifle that has an ability to accept a detachable magazine and has at least two of the following: a folding or telescoping stock; a pistol grip that protrudes conspicuously beneath the action of the weapon; a bayonet mount; a flash suppressor or threaded barrel; and a grenade launcher.

- A semi-automatic pistol that has an ability to accept a detachable magazine and has at least two of the following: an ammunition magazine that attaches to the pistol outside of the pistol grip; a threaded barrel capable of accepting a barrel extender, flash suppressor, forward hand-grip, or silencer; a shroud that is attached to, or partially or completely encircles, the barrel and that permits the shooter to hold the firearm with the nontrigger hand without being burned; a manufactured weight of 50 ounces or more when the pistol is unloaded; and a semiautomatic version of an automatic firearm.

- A semi-automatic shotgun that has at least two of the following: a folding or telescoping stock; a pistol grip that protrudes conspicuously beneath the action of the weapon; a fixed magazine in excess of five rounds; and an ability to accept a detachable magazine.

have created an easy way for manufacturers to copy existing assault weapons and sell the copies legally. Despite this wording, some manufacturers have produced close reproductions of banned assault weapons with one or two modifications in an attempt to work around the letter of the law.

The law does not apply to all guns; those designed for use in hunting and recreational activities are not affected. Addressing concerns that weapons would be taken away from hunters and sporting shooters, the law specifically protects 670 types of hunting rifles and shotguns. The list is not exhaustive, and a gun does not have to be on the list to be protected.

Opponents of the Assault Weapons Ban felt that the guns were being targeted because of design features that only *appear* menacing and that these features are really no more dangerous than are those of any other type of firearm. However, the bill's authors claim that the menacing features—such as silencers, folding stocks, and bayonets—really do make the weapons more dangerous. Such additions are designed for military combat, they say, and make it easier for the firearm user to kill more people in less time. Gun control advocates say the ban acknowledges the difference between semiautomatic rifles used for sports and hunting and "assault weapons" designed with military use in mind. Semiautomatic hunting rifles are designed to be fired from the shoulder, and their effectiveness depends on the accuracy of a precisely aimed projectile; semiautomatic assault weapons are designed to maximize lethal effects through a rapid rate of fire. They are spray-fired from the hip, so a shooter can control the weapon with one hand while firing a large amount of ammunition.

Loopholes make existing gun laws ineffective.

On April 20, 1999, Dylan Klebold and Eric Harris opened fire on their classmates at Columbine High School in Littleton, Colorado. The two 17-year-old boys were armed with home-made bombs, a semiautomatic carbine, a semiautomatic pistol, and two sawed-off shotguns. They killed 12 students and one teacher and injured nearly two dozen others before committing suicide. Robyn Anderson, an 18-year-old friend of the two students, had purchased two of the four weapons used in the massacre, no questions asked, from private sellers at the Tanner Gun Show near Denver. Had a background check been required, Anderson later said, she never would have made the purchase.

> **What other liberty-versus-danger issues are argued about as guns are?**
>
> **Could all these debates be resolved through a single compromise or set of compromises?**

It is difficult to find statistics on gun control in the United States. Many existing laws are so fraught with loopholes, advocates say, that their effectiveness is impossible to measure. The gun show loophole may be the most notorious. Gun shows were originally fairs put on to display new models and showcase rare curios. In the 1960s and 1970s, as the firearm industry expanded and gun ownership increased, the gun show became a popular venue for simply selling firearms. The 2,000 to 5,000 gun shows held each year in the United States began to attract those seeking to buy guns in anonymity.[13] Even under the Brady Act, which requires licensed gun dealers to run background checks on all sales, unlicensed dealers can sell firearms at gun shows, and in 32 states, background checks are not required. Gun control activists believe the gun shows make it easier for guns to end up in the hands of unqualified owners.

> **Do gun controls do anything to stop the first-time criminal?**

Sales by unlicensed dealers, in addition to not being subject to background checks, pose a problem for law enforcement. These purchases are nearly impossible to trace because no records are kept of the sale. Several versions of bills requiring background checks on private and gun show firearms sales had been proposed to Congress by late 2002.

Pro-control groups argue that allowing guns in the household creates a problem of policy—namely, that there is no easy way to ensure that children, and other people who by law may not possess guns, will not have access to them. Moderate pro-control groups propose trigger locks and other safety devices to mitigate this problem; anti-control groups counter that this danger can best be reduced through education.

Guns make homes more dangerous.

When a gun is used in self-defense, the potential victim's chances of staying alive are usually increased. What gun control opponents don't point out is that victims don't usually have time to reach their firearms during an attack. More important, advocates argue, is that guns kept at home for self-defense are more likely to be used in a suicide, accidental death, or homicide than in protecting the owner. Very few murders are the result of a burglary attempt or other felony. Rather, most homicides follow arguments, often among people who know each other.

Approximately one third of all female murder victims considered in a 1995 Bureau of Justice Statistics study had been killed by someone they'd known.[14]

Gun control advocates say that by encouraging people to buy handguns for self-defense the gun industry is perpetrating a dangerous fearfulness, one that causes more deaths than it saves.

How can a gun be kept safely in the household?

"This spiral of violence—buying handguns to protect ourselves from other people with handguns—fuels gun death and injury in the United States. This is because the handgun bought for self-protection is far more likely to be used against the owner or someone known to the owner—in a homicide (usually as the result of an argument), a suicide, or an unintentional shooting—than in legitimate self-defense."[15]

Gun control advocates believe that guns in the home pose more risks than they avoid. Keeping a gun at home increases the risk of being murdered by a family member or close friend by nearly three times. In addition to increasing the risk of homicide, guns in the home can increase the risk of suicide: Guns were two times more likely to be found in the homes of adolescents who committed suicide than in the homes of those who unsuccessfully attempted suicide. Some research has shown that suicide is nearly five times more likely in homes with firearms.

Between 1980 and 1992, suicide rates rose among people between the ages of 10 and 19 years, among young African-American men, and among elderly men of all races. Firearms accounted for 77 percent of the increase in suicides from 1980 to 1992 and were disproportionately responsible for the increases among youth and the elderly. In line with historical precedent, western states had the highest rates of suicide. Firearms accounted for many of the geographic differences in suicide rates and explained much of the increase in several states.

In 1984, Bernhard Goetz sparked a national debate on concealed weapons when he shot four teenagers who threatened him on a New York subway. Some applauded Goetz's actions, seeing the event as evidence that handguns are useful or necessary for self-defense. Others feel that Goetz went too far and worry that an abundance of firearms will lead to unjustifiable violence.

Concealed weapons mean concealed risk.

Many of the events that catalyze renewed interest in gun control become tools for both sides in the debate. The case of Bernhard Goetz is such an example. His story proves that it can be hard to differentiate between aggression and self-defense.

On Dec. 22, 1984, four African-American boys in their teens approached Bernhard Goetz on a New York City subway and asked for money. The 37-year-old Goetz, an electrical engineer, had been mugged twice before, and the boys were holding screwdrivers. Goetz panicked. Taking a silver-plated .38-caliber revolver from his coat, he shot and wounded all four of them. Goetz fled but surrendered to police in Concord,

New Hampshire, where he confessed to the shooting and to having acted "viciously and savagely." Goetz admitted to police that he told one of the men he shot, Darrell Cabey, "You don't look so bad. Here's another," and shot him again, in the spine, crippling the youth for life. Arguing that he had acted in self-defense, Goetz was later acquitted by a jury on charges of attempted-murder and assault. He was sentenced to an eight-month jail term for possessing a concealed gun without a permit.

The Goetz case became international news. Goetz was called "the Subway Vigilante." Some people thought he was a hero for having the nerve to defend himself. Others thought he was a violent menace who was motivated by fear and racism.

Gun rights groups have continued to champion Goetz as a poster child for the campaign to liberalize concealed weapons laws. Whether Goetz would have or could have gotten a concealed carry permit, gun rights groups believe he is living proof of the value of carrying firearms for self-protection. Given the very real danger of violent crime, they say, Goetz not only saved his own life but may also have struck fear in the hearts of criminals. Gun control advocates, however, see a warning in his story: If people are allowed, or encouraged, to carry guns at all times, they argue, average people who are afraid, racist, angry, or intoxicated would be more likely to gun down the people around them.

> **Did Bernhard Goetz go too far?**
>
> **Do Goetz's actions threaten the legitimacy of carrying weapons for self-defense?**

The United States has a notoriously high rate of handgun deaths, for which many anti-gun advocates blame permissive gun ownership laws. Other countries with stricter gun laws have lower gun death rates. The trouble in the United States is not with lax enforcement of existing laws: restrictions in effect now have too many loopholes. The Brady Act's background check requirement has had some crime-reducing effect, and so has the federal assault weapons law, but these still do not meaningfully prevent criminals from buying guns informally or at gun shows. Meanwhile, gun control advocates argue that keeping weapons for self-defense is actually dangerous to the gun owner's own household. They say the mentality of preparation for violent self-defense makes nobody safer and causes a continuing cycle of violence.

Gun Control Does Not Prevent Crime

Everyone has heard the NRA mantra, "Guns don't kill people—*people* kill people." The idea that guns themselves do not cause gun violence is a fundamental element of the argument against gun control. Most gun owners never use their weapons in crimes, and only a small fraction of guns are used illegally.[1] Despite a mostly steady increase in gun ownership during the 20th century, crime rates went up and down. With thousands of gun laws that are already unenforced, gun rights advocates ask what good it will do to pass more. The idea is this: Easy access to guns is not the driving force behind crime. There must be something else.

Guns aren't the reason for crime.

Many critics of gun control believe that guns have very little to do with the unusual amount of violent death in the United

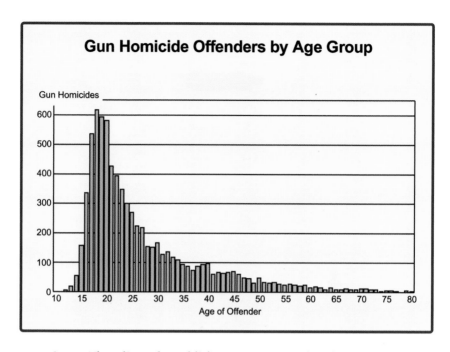

Gun Homicide Offenders by Age Group

Gun Homicides

Age of Offender

States. They direct the public's attention instead to the decline in religious observance, the erosion of traditional family values, and the prevalence of violence in movies and music. Gun control critics say the key to reducing crime lies in the laws already on the books, from drug laws to gun laws. Gun control opponents say that the 20,000-plus gun laws on the books in states and municipalities are underenforced. By increasing enforcement, they say, police and prosecutors could reduce crime without the added confusion of more legislation. In this analysis, they often use successful crime crackdowns in New York and other major cities in the 1990s as examples.

New York has the oldest handgun licensing law in the United States: the Sullivan Act of 1911. Nonetheless, the city had one of the highest violent crime rates in the country from the 1960s through the 1990s. In the mid-1990s, the New York City Police Department began a massive law enforcement push that focused on eliminating "quality of life" crimes, such as graffiti and loitering; limiting the number of vendors selling pornography; and cracking down on drug crimes. Gun control opponents say that it was good police work, not more laws, that reduced crime in New York City.

Another way to look at the impact of better enforcement is to examine crime rates in states where increased enforcement has led to higher prison populations. Between 1980 and 1994, the 10 states with the largest increases in prison population experienced a drop in violent crime by an average of 13 percent, whereas the 10 states with the smallest increases in prison population experienced an average 55 percent increase in violent crime.[2]

> **Would public money be better directed toward punishing/rehabilitating people who break laws or toward preventing people from breaking laws in the first place?**
>
> **What is the best way to stop people from breaking a law?**

Gun control opponents also point to high crime rates in cities and states that have taken extreme measures to limit access to firearms. Their conclusion is that the controls, although onerous, had little effect on crime. The NRA website points to efforts in Washington, D.C.; Chicago; New York; Maryland; and California. Washington, D.C. banned handgun sales in 1977, as did Chicago in 1982. By the early 1990s, the homicide rate had tripled in Washington, D.C. and had doubled in Chicago. Chicago had imposed a registration requirement for handguns in 1968 and nevertheless saw rising handgun-related homicide rates.

California, a historical testing ground for gun control, raised the waiting period on handgun sales from 5 to 15 days in 1975 (the waiting period has since been reduced to 10 days), passed an assault weapons ban in 1989, and in 1990 imposed the waiting period on rifles and shotguns. However, the state's annual homicide rate remains an average 34 percent higher than the rate for the rest of the country.

Maryland has also imposed extensive restrictions on firearms ownership, including a waiting period; a gun purchase limit; a ban on cheap, compact, small-caliber guns (often called "junk guns" or "Saturday Night Specials"); restrictions on some assault weapons; and state regulation of the nonlicensed transfers of firearms. Nevertheless, the state's homicide rate is, on average, 46 percent higher than the rate for the rest of the country.

> **What can be done to stop the flow of weapons into places where ownership is restricted?**

According to the NRA, the combined homicide rate for the six jurisdictions with the most restrictive firearms policies — California, Illinois, Maryland, New Jersey, New York, and Washington, D.C. — is 23 percent higher than the rate for the rest of the country. In the view of the NRA, the relationship between high murder rates and strong gun control in these states is clear: gun control does nothing to prevent crime and may even encourage it.

The NRA also contests assertions by gun control advocates that the major gun laws of the 20th century — the Brady Act, the Assault Weapons Ban, and the Gun Control Act of 1968 — measurably reduced crime rates.[3]

Until the passage of the Brady Act and the federal Assault Weapons Ban, the Gun Control Act of 1968 (GCA) was the nation's most extensive gun control legislation. The GCA required gun manufacturers and dealers to obtain licenses and prohibited certain groups, such as felons and people with diminished mental capacity, from purchasing guns. The NRA quotes statistics from the years before and after the GCA that show that crime rates were lower before the bill went into effect. The national homicide rate was 50 percent higher, on average, during the five years after the law than during the five years before it. Ten years later, the rate was, on average, 81 percent higher.

Gun control advocates claim that the 1993 Brady Act, which required background checks and waiting periods for gun purchases, has reduced violent crime and murder rates. Critics respond with statistics, such as a study published in *Journal of*

THE LETTER OF THE LAW

The Gun Control Act of 1968 (GCA)

The Gun Control Act of 1968 (GCA) was pushed through Congress in response to the political assassinations of Dr. Martin Luther King, Jr. and presidential candidate Senator Robert Kennedy.

The main goal of the GCA was to create categories of "prohibited purchasers," groups of people not legally entitled to possess firearms because of age, criminal background, or incompetence. The prohibited groups include convicted felons, fugitives from justice, illegal drug users or addicts, minors, anyone adjudicated mentally defective or having been committed to a mental institution, anyone dishonorably discharged from the military, illegal aliens, and anyone having renounced U.S. citizenship. The law also established a system for licensing dealers, manufacturers, and distributors.

In addition, the law

- Requires serial numbers on all firearms.

- Prohibits the interstate sale of firearms.

- Requires handgun purchasers to buy their guns in the state in which they reside. (Today, long guns may be purchased from gun dealers in any state, regardless of purchaser's state of residence.)

- Sets minimal ages for firearms purchasers: Handgun purchasers must be at least 21. Long gun purchasers must be at least 18.

- Prohibits the importation of nonsporting weapons such as the Saturday Night Special, some semiautomatic assault rifles, and certain military weapons.

- Bans mail-order sales of firearms and ammunition.

- Sets penalties for use of firearms in crimes of violence or drug trafficking.

- Prohibits importation of foreign-made military surplus firearms.

- Prohibits the sale and manufacture of new fully automatic civilian machine guns.

- Prohibits the sale of parts or "conversion kits" used to make semiautomatic firearms fully automatic.

the American Medical Association, that negate the impact of the new law. In August of 2000, the journal reported that states implementing waiting periods and background checks did "not [experience] reductions in homicide rates or overall suicide rates."[4]

Gun control puts guns into the hands of criminals.

Another major tenet of the anti–gun control argument is that gun control will limit only law-abiding citizens' access to guns. Increased regulations, it is said, may in fact catalyze the formation of a black market for guns, increasing the availability of firearms that are unchecked by the gun control system. An apt historical comparison can be found in the surge of bootlegging and illegal saloons, or speakeasies, during the 1920s, when the 18th Amendment to the Constitution prohibited the consumption of alcohol. Gun control proposals would erect a series of barriers to gun ownership: waiting periods, background checks, licensing tests, and paperwork for registration. Although responsible sport and hunting gun users struggle with new bureaucratic hurdles, critics say, it will be nearly impossible to make *criminals* comply. If only criminals and police have guns, control opponents say, cities and suburbs will become much more dangerous. Average people, without access to guns, will be more vulnerable than they are today.

There is also a potential problem with size and scope: With more than 220 million firearms in circulation, gun rights groups say it would be impossible to significantly reduce the number of guns that can enter the black market. Gun control laws affect only legal sales. Because an estimated 80 percent of firearms used in crimes are traded

How can a "black market" be controlled through legislation?

through illegal or unregulated means, control opponents say, stricter laws enforced on legal markets will ensure that only criminals have access to guns.

A collection of weapons seized by U.S. government agents. Opponents of gun control argue that "if guns are outlawed, then only outlaws will have guns" and that legal gun ownership is necessary to control crime; proponents of gun control argue in return that giving citizens access to guns like these will do more harm than good.

International comparisons are misleading.

Gun control advocates often cite the low rates of crime in certain areas that enforce strict gun control laws, such as England, Italy, and Japan. Gun control opponents counter with statistics from Switzerland, Israel, and Norway. Gun ownership is high among the last three, where gun-related crime rates are comparable with or lower than those in England, Italy, and Japan. Most Swiss adults, as members of the national militia, keep government-issued fully automatic rifles and ammunition in their homes. The Swiss government, which maintains a position of neutrality in international affairs, sees arming its citizenry as a method of protecting against foreign attack.

Gun control opponents believe that international comparisons

(1) fail to take into account cultural differences that may influence crime rates and (2) give too much credit to the role of gun control in limiting crime. The presence of gun control laws, they say, doesn't reliably predict whether crime rates are high or low in foreign countries, and so the regulations can't be relied on to solve the United States' problems with crime. Of course, this recalls the central argument that guns are not responsible for crime.

Attorney Don B. Kates, whose work includes Second Amendment issues, wrote, "In any society, truly violent people are only a small minority. We know that law-abiding citizens do not commit violent crimes. We know that criminals will neither obey gun bans nor refrain from turning other deadly instruments to their nefarious purposes. . . . In sum, peaceful societies do not need general gun bans and violent societies do not benefit from them."[5]

Self-defense reduces crime.

Perhaps the most compelling tactic in the debate over gun control concerns self-defense. Handgun owners consistently report defense against attackers as the chief reason for their purchase of a firearm. The media's attention to crime and real statistics on burglary make the incentives for this motivation clear: U.S. citizens are afraid of violent crime. In the belief that police cannot guard against every break-in and assault, many U.S. citizens purchase firearms to protect their families.

Critics of gun control believe that many U.S. citizens not only want access to self-defense but also take action in self-defense. When would-be victims use a firearm in self-defense, they say, fewer crimes are successful. Thus, if gun control laws prevent people from protecting themselves by reducing access to guns, the laws allow some crimes to occur that might have been prevented had the restrictions not been in place.

Analysts in the anti–gun control camp have focused on the number of cases in which guns are actually used to stop crimes

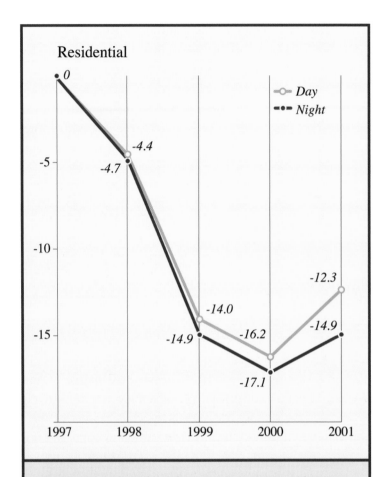

Changes in residential burglary rates (in percentage) between 1997 and 2001. The drop in these rates was steep until 2000, when the rates began to rise once again. Anti-control groups use the rising rates as evidence that guns are necessary to protect households, but pro-control groups point out that the rates remain significantly below those of 1997 and may fall again.

in action. In statistical studies, it has been shown that when a gun is used in self-defense the victim's chances of surviving increase. Although the statistics are highly contested, gun control opponents such as criminologists Gary Kleck and

Marc Gertz have presented statistics showing an estimated 2.5 million defensive uses of firearms each year.[6] This is three to five times the estimated number of violent crimes committed with firearms annually.

Criminologist John Lott took this point a step further, arguing that increased gun ownership may actually reduce crime by serving as a deterrent to criminals. Lott's research measured the impact on crime rates of increased gun ownership and increased access to carrying concealed weapons. He put forward controversial studies that show that in certain communities, when more people own guns, the rate of violent crime decreases.[7] This hypothesis is very controversial because it asserts as fact the exact opposite of what gun control advocates have maintained for years. Instead of arguing that gun control won't work very well, or is unenforceable, it suggests that gun control might actually make crime rates increase.

What is the effect of strict gun regulation on crime?

Is this due more to the *degree* of regulation or to the *type* of regulation?

Gun control opponents point to national and local statistics that show lower crime rates after reductions in gun control and greater access to weapons.

In 1982, Kennesaw, Georgia passed an unprecedented new ordinance that required the heads of households, with some exceptions, to keep ammunition and at least one firearm in the house. For the next five years, burglaries fell by 89 percent.[8] Although the ordinance may not have actually increased gun ownership, gun rights groups say a clear message still rang clear: "[A]ny homeowner confronted during a burglary would almost certainly be armed."[9]

A highly publicized safety course that taught women in Orlando, Florida how to use guns in 1966 and 1967 was followed by a drop of 88 percent in rape rates. A 1979 Justice Department study found that 32 percent of attempted rapes

Did the Florida experience "scare off" potential rapists?

What might the statistic mean by "rape rates"?

Is it likely that the self-defense course reduced the incidence of *all* varieties of rape?

were successful. When the potential victim was armed with a gun or knife, the success rate of attempted rapes dropped to 3 percent.[10]

Concealed weapons reduce crime.

These studies centered on communities that had liberalized their concealed-weapons laws. Concealed-carry weapons laws (CCWs) allow people to carry guns concealed on their person in public. They apply to a woman who carries a ".22" in her purse for self-protection and to a would-be criminal who hides a licensed handgun under his trenchcoat. The NRA began a campaign to pass lenient concealed-carry laws in the 1980s. Some existing laws, the so-called "may issue" laws, allowed local police to make the final decision in granting a concealed-weapon permit to an applicant that met certain qualifications. The NRA lobbied state legislatures to change the "may issue" laws into "*shall* issue" laws, which would force local police to grant a permit to any applicant who met a basic list of criteria.

In his book *More Guns, Less Crime*, Lott cites statistics from

Justifiable Homicide
by Weapon, Private Citizen, 1997-2001

Year	Total	Total fire-arms	Hand-guns	Rifles	Shot-guns	Fire-arms, type not stated	Knives or cutting instru-ments	Other danger-ous weapons	Personal weapons
1997	280	238	197	16	14	11	28	6	8
1998	196	170	150	6	14	0	17	5	4
1999	192	158	137	5	10	6	18	9	7
2000	164	138	123	4	7	4	15	8	3
2001	215	176	136	10	13	17	25	6	8

the late 1980s and early 1990s, when rising gun ownership accompanied falling national crime rates. He says the states with the largest drops in crime, at the time, were also the states with the "fastest growing percentages of gun ownership." He argues that in states that have passed more lenient concealed-carry laws, murder and crime rates dropped. According to his review of statistics in all U.S. counties from 1977 to 1992, states that passed concealed-carry laws reduced their rates of murder by 8.5 percent, rape by 5 percent, aggravated assault by 7 percent, and robbery by 3 percent.

"Many factors influence crime," Lott writes, "with arrest and conviction rates being the most important. However, nondiscretionary concealed-handgun laws are also important, and they are the most cost-effective means of reducing crime."[11]

Lott bases his argument on the logical assumption that criminals take the easiest route possible. If certain crimes, such as armed robbery, become more difficult—perhaps because more citizens are armed— then the criminals will attempt them less frequently. Gun ownership, Lott contends, is therefore a method of

Is Lott's assumption about criminals valid?

deterring crime. "Allowing citizens to carry concealed handguns reduces violent crimes," Lott declares; "mass shootings in public places are reduced when law abiding citizens are allowed to carry concealed handguns."

Gun rights activists rely on survey data showing that criminals are less likely to break the law if they suspect citizens are armed. According to a Justice Department study, three fifths of felons polled agreed that "a criminal is not going to mess around with a victim he knows is armed with a gun." Nearly 75 percent of felons polled agreed that "one reason burglars avoid houses when people are at home is that they fear being shot during the crime." Fifty-seven percent of felons polled agreed that "criminals are more worried about meeting an armed victim than they are about running into the police."[13]

James Brady, injured in a 1981 assassination attempt on President Ronald Reagan, has called for sweeping gun control legislation, including mandatory use of safety locks that prevent children from using handguns. Recently, some manufacturers, wary of liability lawsuits, also have advocated safety devices. Some opponents to gun control argue that these safety devices reduce a firearm's usefulness for self-defense.

"Safety" features are dangerous in their own right.

If self-defense is one of the main reasons for owning a handgun, it follows that anything designed to make guns less accessible would be opposed by gun owners. Therefore, opponents believe that safety precautions, such as storing guns unloaded and using trigger locks, reduce the usefulness of firearms as tools for self-defense. Trigger locks and unloaded storing measures make it much less likely that potential victims would be able to unlock and load their weapons quickly enough to protect themselves during an attack. Opponents also argue that these safety measures reduce the usefulness of firearms as passive crime deterrents. A gun serves as a deterrent, many owners contend, because criminals may fear the consequences of attacking a public that is likely to be armed. By making it harder for citizens to use their weapons, these "safety" precautions could actually make criminals feel less vulnerable when committing crimes. Opponents believe the law should allow gun owners to store their weapons in the most easily accessible fashion possible: loaded and within reach.

Targeted bans are a dangerous step toward total gun prohibition.

Since the early 1970s, campaigns have come and gone for targeted bans on Saturday Night Specials, "cop-killer bullets," "assault rifles," and plastic guns. Activists for gun availability fear that these limited restrictions are merely a way to open a back door to more prohibitionist bans that target all or most firearms. The NRA and other gun rights groups believe the aim of all gun control policies is the outright prohibition of firearms.

The movement to enact targeted bans on handguns began in the 1970s. A 1972 Senate bill, which ultimately failed, would have restricted the production of Saturday Night Specials, guns that were inexpensive and likely to be used by criminals. Broader restrictions on handguns were sought in the 1980s, especially after the assassination attempt on President Ronald Reagan. Believing these targeted efforts would eventually lead to a mass movement to ban all guns, the NRA and other groups responded in force. They defended handguns as tools for self-defense. Most people who buy firearms for protection choose handguns. According to research by criminologist Gary Kleck, small handguns such as the Saturday Night Special are probably more

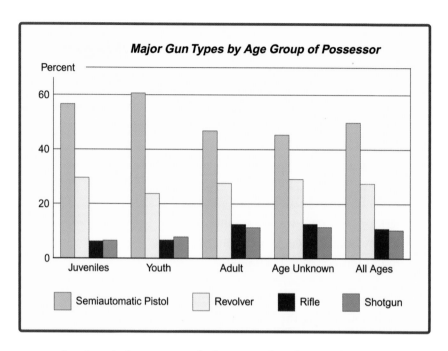

Major Gun Types by Age Group of Possessor

Percent

60

40

20

0

Juveniles   Youth   Adult   Age Unknown   All Ages

Semiautomatic Pistol   Revolver   Rifle   Shotgun

often bought by poor people for protection than used in crimes. Bans on such guns, Kleck writes, "would have their greatest impact in reducing the availability of defensive handguns to low-income people."[14]

The focus turned to assault weapons in the late 1980s. The Assault Weapons Ban, part of the Violent Crime Control and Law Enforcement Act, was passed in 1994. Gun rights activists staged a heavy opposition to the bill. They say the act restricts the loosely defined category of assault weapons because the guns *look* scary and not because they pose a greater threat. They also say the bans are difficult to define, a criticism they apply to almost all gun control policies. A definition of a Saturday Night Special could be as narrow as a detailed quality checklist or as broad as "all handguns shorter than four inches." Assault rifles are even more difficult to define. The military-style design features that characterize such guns don't necessarily make them more dangerous, according to the NRA. Opponents say it is nearly impossible to come up with an effective legal definition of assault weapons, and therefore the law is a hodgepodge of directed bans that could potentially restrict guns popular for legal hunting and sporting events.

They also argue that assault weapons, however they are defined, are rarely involved in crimes. This fact, they argue, exposes the political motivations of gun control advocates. In addition, even banned assault weapons are still relatively easy to purchase because firearms manufacturers flooded the market with extra guns before the ban went into effect. Gun manufacturers also found ways to produce guns with a few modifications that would meet the requirements of the ban.

Gun advocates argue that there are many reasons for crime other than gun availability, a fact that makes international comparisons misleading. They say restricting guns is not an effective way to fight crime, and, on the contrary, encouraging gun possession, including the carrying of concealed weapons, can have the effect of discouraging crime. Making a "slippery slope" argument, gun advocates further argue that safety measures such as trigger locks make guns less readily available for self-defense and that limiting a particular kind of gun, such as the "Saturday Night Special," is a step toward banning guns entirely.

Gun Manufacturers Should Be Held Financially Responsible for Gun-Related Deaths

In 1999, there were 28,874 gun-related deaths in the United States; in 2000, there were 28,663.[1] These were the first two years in nearly two decades in which the number had fallen below 30,000—a decline too small for most to consider a victory. Gun violence, like all causes of injury and death, has an economic impact on families and government. Gunshot wounds cost thousands of dollars to treat. The average cost of a gun-related crime may be as high as $268,000.[2] The American College of Physicians estimates that, in the aggregate, the direct cost of firearms injuries is more than $4 billion

If one person unknowingly provides the means of harming another, is that person responsible for the harm?

Can gun manufacturers assume that their products will be used for murder and other crimes?

per year,[3] with $19 billion in additional harm such as lost potential earnings.[4]

Because the United States does not have nationalized health care, cities, states, and counties are often left with the burden of providing emergency care to victims of gun violence who cannot afford medical attention on their own. Gun violence necessitates millions more in spending on police, courts, prisons, and school security.

Guns are the only consumer products *designed* to injure or kill. Gun control advocates posit this question: The makers of other dangerous products—cars, drugs, and machinery— are held to strict safety guidelines. Why not gun manufacturers?

Starting in 1998 with Chicago and New Orleans, U.S. cities and counties began filing suits against gun manufacturers for damages from the negative impact of gun violence in their communities. Most of the suits target both manufacturers and gun sellers, blaming the gun makers for producing and marketing a dangerous product and blaming dealers for distributing the product unethically. The suits rest on the legal concept of liability: the idea that when a person or entity fails in a responsibility or duty to another person or group, that duty can be enforced with a variety of punishments, including monetary damages paid to those who suffer. Late in 2002, it was still unclear how successful the suits would be. The gun industry was buoyed by early court support for its position, but that support was less universal among district and circuit courts four years after the first cases surfaced. Many appellate courts allowed the suits to proceed.

There is strong public support for holding manufacturers responsible.

The impetus for the dozens of lawsuits against gun manufacturers is often traced to the tragic death of a young boy on the streets of Chicago in 1996. Stephen Young's son was killed by a bullet fired out of a speeding car by a reputed Latin Kings gang member. The gunman was wielding a Bryco 9-mm semiautomatic handgun

Murder Victims
by Weapon, 1997-2001

Weapons	1997	1998	1999	2000	2001
Total	15,837	14,276	13,011	13,230	13,752
Total firearms:	10,729	9,257	8,480	8,661	8,719
Handguns	8,441	7,430	6,658	6,778	6,790
Rifles	638	548	400	411	389
Shotguns	643	633	531	485	497
Other guns	35	16	92	53	58
Firearms, type not stated	972	630	799	934	985
Knives or cutting instruments	2,055	1,899	1,712	1,782	1,796
Blunt objects (clubs, hammers, etc.)	724	755	756	617	661
Personal weapons (hands, fists, feet, etc.)	1,010	964	885	927	925
Poison	6	6	11	8	10
Explosives	8	10	0	9	4
Fire	140	132	133	134	104
Narcotics	37	35	26	20	34
Drowning	34	28	28	15	23
Strangulation	224	213	190	166	152
Asphyxiation	88	101	106	92	112
Other weapons or weapons not stated	782	876	684	799	1,212

that had been bought along with 40 other weapons during a single purchase in a suburban gun shop. Known as "straw buys," such purchases are organized by middlemen who buy large stocks of weapons from licensed dealers and then resell the guns to criminals who can't legally purchase firearms.

What can be done about straw buys?

Stephen Young was furious and decided to do something about it. He, along with three other Chicago families, filed suit against gun manufacturers, seeking damages for the loss of their loved ones. The suit alleged malfeasance on the part of the gun industry for designing certain weapons with a criminal's taste in mind, such as short revolvers that can easily be hidden under a shirt. It accused companies of marketing their products directly to criminals by touting handy attributes, like the TEC-DC9 assault rifle's resistance to fingerprints.

Inspired by Young's suit against the industry, which was still pending in the appellate system in late 2002, the City of Chicago made its own claim against the industry. On November 12, 1998, the City of Chicago and Cook County filed a lawsuit against 23 gun manufacturers, 12 local gun dealers, and numerous intermediary gun distributors.

Is it likely that relatives of murder victims are suing gun manufacturers simply because the murderers themselves do not have much money?

The lawsuit is based partially on an undercover operation that unearthed a vast network of illegal gun trafficking from less strictly regulated areas outside Chicago into the inner city, where handguns and assault weapons are strictly limited. Over a three-month period, undercover officers from the Chicago Police Department attempted to purchase weapons from the 12 gun stores around Chicago that had sold the highest numbers of guns traced to crimes in the city. The agents presented store clerks with Chicago identification. It was a clear sign that these "customers" wanted to break the law: Chicago residents are prohibited from purchasing the firearms the agents were attempting to buy. In their interactions with store owners, the agents boasted about the criminal purposes for the weapons: selling the guns to gangs or "settling a score." Nonetheless, they walked away with 171 guns and advice from many dealers on how to avoid federal legal requirements in making the purchases.

Chicago was soon joined by dozens of other cities and states seeking damages from the $2 billion gun industry for failing to produce and market its products responsibly. The lawsuits seek also to force industry reform. Gun control advocates hope the gun makers will begin making safer guns and endorsing sensible controls. The cities have used a variety of strategies in designing their suits against the industry. The cases are built around three main ideas: unsafe gun design, negligent distribution, and deceptive marketing and advertising.

Gun designs are often unsafe.

Many of the lawsuits incorporate arguments that gun makers ignored the likely and preventable misuse of their products and failed to make safe weapons. This tactic relies upon state statutes under which well-functioning products can be deemed defective if they are unreasonably dangerous in design. These suits assert that locking systems and "smart gun" technology are available but gun makers choose not to use them. Manufacturers have also been slow to incorporate "magazine disconnect safeties" or "'chamber loaded' indicators," which can notify handlers if a gun is ready to fire ammunition. This tactic follows suits against car makers who fail to install seatbelts or airbags. In addition to seeking damages, these suits are aimed at changing designs for future weapon production.

> **What is the difference between suing a car company for accidents caused by faulty brakes and suing a gun company for murders committed with guns that work just as designed?**

Manufacturers do not monitor the distribution of guns effectively.

The lawsuits also usually assail the gun industry for distributing their products negligently, in a manner that jeopardizes communities. This tactic addresses the alleged failure of the gun industry to monitor and control the sales practices of gun distributors and dealers. Lawyers argue that, without any oversight, dealers knowingly sell guns into a secondary market in which legally purchased firearms are resold at street level to criminals and others who can't legally buy them. The suits accuse the industry of flooding markets with lax gun control with the full intention of letting the guns filter through illegal markets into neighboring communities with strict gun laws. Communities that have filed these suits aim to tighten distribution practices and keep guns out of criminals' hands.

Gun manufacturers have defended against lawsuits by claiming that gun sales are closely regulated. However, at gun shows like the one these people just attended, the standards for gun sales are less strict. Gun shows can act as a black market, providing guns to people who by law should not have access to them.

Manufacturers and dealers conceal the danger of guns.

Many of the cities have also asserted claims that the gun industry has engaged in deceptive marketing practices. By advancing arguments that guns make homes safer, these suits contend, the gun industry has lied to consumers. Gun control advocates have long held that a gun is far more likely to kill or injure a household member than an intruder, and a gun's presence in a home greatly increases the chances of a homicide, suicide, or accidental death.

If a private chain, such as Wal-Mart, institutes safeguards for gun sales, is it violating peoples' rights?

Gun control advocates have bristled at attempts by the NRA and industry groups to block lawsuits with legislative measures. More than 30 states have passed laws that ban localities from filing liability suits against gun makers, and a similar federal bill is making headway in Congress. Control advocates accuse legislators of protecting the gun industry. The Violence Policy Center's Kristen Rand writes of the federal legislation now in Congress, "This misguided legislation would protect the manufacturers of the assault weapons used in the April 20, 1999, Columbine massacre in Littleton, CO: the

Gun-Related Federal Offenses

Gun control tends to fall to the specifications of individual states, but federal law does "put its foot down" on a number of points. Gun-related crimes that have been designated as federal offenses include:

- Lying to a licensed dealer in order to buy a gun [18 U.S.C. §922(a)(6)]

- Stealing a gun [18 U.S.C. §§922(u), 924(k), 924(l)] or handling or transporting a stolen gun [18 U.S.C. §922(j)] or a gun whose serial number has been erased [18 U.S.C. §922(k)]

- Selling or giving a gun to anyone under the age of 18 [18 U.S.C. §922(x)], being in possession of a gun in a school zone, regardless of age [18 U.S.C. §922(q)], and being a minor and having a gun, regardless of how it was acquired [18 U.S.C. 922(k)]

TEC-DC9 assault pistol and the Hi-Point Carbine. Instead of protecting communities from gun violence, Congress is working to protect gun manufacturers' bottom line."[5]

Gun retailers, who are often implicated when cities take manufacturers to court, are beginning to explore their options. The world's largest retail chain, Wal-Mart Stores, Inc., decided in the summer of 2002 to make screenings of gun purchases at its stores more thorough, taking an extra step beyond the federal background check requirements. The chain, which sells firearms in most of its 2,700 stores, now prohibits sales until potential buyers have been approved by the appropriate federal or state agency. Under current Brady Act regulations, a gun sale can proceed if the government fails to finish its background check within three business days. Wal-Mart was immediately criticized by the NRA, which accused the chain of interfering with citizens' Second Amendment rights. NRA spokesman Andrew Arulanandam said Wal-Mart's new policy "penalizes law-abiding citizens."[6] Ultimately, under pressure from members who supported Wal-Mart's decision, the NRA decided to work with the chain to improve the background check system.

———————————•———————•———————•———————————

Cities and individuals affected by gun violence have begun to bring lawsuits against gun manufacturers, seeking to hold them responsible for the criminal use of their products. From the cities' point of view, gun violence forces them to spend money on health care and other services, and so the companies that make guns available to criminals should help pay for the damage. Principal theories of liability in their complaints have included unsafe design, negligent distribution, and deceptive marketing and advertising. While these lawsuits have had mixed success, their pressure has pushed some gun retailers, including Wal-Mart, to screen their customers more cautiously.

Gun Manufacturers Are Not Responsible for Gun-Related Deaths

There is no legal basis for liability.

Gun manufacturers dismiss the liability suits as fundamentally flawed; they say they produce a legal product and cannot be expected to control how people use firearms any more than auto makers can control how people drive.

Industry lawyers have some advantages in designing their defense. To begin with, gun makers never promised the public that their products were safe. The dangerous and lethal capabilities of guns were always acknowledged and sometimes even trumpeted.

Because the plaintiffs in the liability lawsuits have used numerous different tactics in arguing their cases, the gun industry, observers say, has an intellectual advantage. Its position has remained the same. Whoever fires a gun, they say, bears full liability for whatever may happen. The gun industry says it cannot hold back the trigger.

Product liability lawsuits are an accepted way of forcing manufacturers to produce safe products. These lawsuits go after companies that build products with clear faults: parts that malfunction and cause injury. Gun industry lobbyists argue that gun-related deaths, however, have nothing to do with product liability. Guns may have been used negligently or with criminal intent, industry spokespeople say, but the guns themselves cannot be blamed. "You don't sue General Motors when someone drives drunk and hurts someone," said Smith & Wesson lawyer Anne Kimball. The gun manufacturers say that going after them distracts from the real problems: crime and social breakdown.

Is it a legitimate defense for gun makers to say that they know their products are dangerous?

If car makers have taken many steps— airbags, additional brakelights, etc.—to make their products safer, why haven't gun manufacturers? Or have they?

What forms might these protections take?

Some suits have attacked the industry for failing to include safety features such as "smart gun" technology that would prevent anyone other than the owner from firing a weapon. However, industry lobbyists say that such technologies are prohibitively expensive and not yet perfected. Gun control opponents say expensive "smart gun" technology would prevent poor people from accessing a tool for self-defense. In a *National Review* article, criminologist John Lott writes, "The futuristic guns advocated in the New Orleans suit . . . are far from reliable and will cost $900 when they are finally available."[1]

Which is more important— human lives or the financial well-being of gun manufacturers?

What if the lives are those of criminals?

What if the manufacturers support thriving local economies?

Is there room for compromise?

Lawsuits against gun manufacturers threaten a legitimate industry.

Some critics have derided the lawsuits as gold-digging expeditions against law-abiding businesses that contribute to the national economy. Representative Chris John (D-La.) warned that "Frivolous lawsuits against gun manufacturers jeopardize a legitimate, legal business that is worth billions of dollars to our national economy."[2]

The NRA has begun pushing for the passage of bills in state legislatures that make it illegal for groups of people or municipalities to sue gun makers for product liability. The NRA has vehemently opposed the shift in the arena of the gun control debate from Congress and state legislatures to the courts. Like other conservative activist groups, the NRA favors legislation over court-set precedent. The group's decision to fight lawsuits with legislation was thus no surprise. Since the first suit was introduced, more than 30 states have enacted NRA-backed legislation that prohibits localities from filing lawsuits; these states include Alabama, Alaska, Arizona, Arkansas, Colorado, Florida, Georgia, Idaho, Indiana, Kansas, Kentucky, Louisiana, Maine, Michigan, Missouri, Montana, Nevada, North Dakota, Ohio, Oklahoma, Pennsylvania, South Carolina, South Dakota, Tennessee, Texas, Utah, Virginia, and Wyoming. On the other hand, California recently legislatively overruled a California Supreme Court decision holding that a 1983 law protected gun manufacturers from suit. The new California legislative action was a response to the 2001 case of *Merrill v. Navegar*, in which the California Supreme Court found a gun manufacturer bore no liability for the actions of a mass murderer who used its products to kill eight people.[3]

If lawsuits against gun manufacturers result in higher gun prices, is this a partial victory?

The NRA supported the introduction of a federal bill, the Protection of Lawful Commerce in Arms Act,[4] in 2001, and the bill was under consideration by committees in both

In this photograph, at an NRA convention, an eight-year-old learns how to aim a handgun. NRA programs teach children how to use guns according to safety guidelines; education is an important part of pro-gun groups' argument for reduced regulation.

the House and the Senate late in 2002. The federal legislation is vital to the industry because state bills are not as effective in preventing lawsuits. In the weeks following the Washington sniper attacks, however, the measure appeared to be stalled, so its future in the remainder of the 2002 session was uncertain.[5]

Jeff Reh, general counsel for Beretta USA Corp., a major American gun manufacturer, gave the following testimony in favor of the federal ban on lawsuits against the industry:

> If the tactic of these lawsuits is allowed to succeed, recourse to the courts can make the legislature superfluous. This violates the Separation of Powers in the Constitution. It also robs the public of their elected voice in government. Regrettably, cases

of this type can succeed, not just through a jury verdict, but because of the costs of defending against litigation. Most firearm manufacturers have small revenues and low profit margins. The tyranny of legal costs can and has driven firearm manufacturers into bankruptcy. Lawsuits put money in the pockets of lawyers rather than in the hands of factory workers. Many countries consider domestic firearm production to be a vital national security interest. These lawsuits threaten that resource in the United States.

Begun to advance one narrow point of view, these cases risk a vital industry. If, for example, a single judge or jurors in one city enter a verdict against the industry in the sum of billions of dollars, the cost of purchasing a bond before an appeal can be undertaken could bankrupt even the most substantial company. Rogue juries or individual judges might see such cases as an opportunity to destroy firearm companies and, either unwittingly or without caring, block the means by which U.S. citizens exercise their Second Amendment freedoms of self-defense and self-determination.[6]

Gun manufacturers also argue that the suits are factually flawed in their argument that the industry has failed to establish regulations that keep guns out of dangerous hands. They argue that the sale and distribution of firearms is, in fact, heavily regulated.

The suit filed by the city of Cincinnati accused gun manufacturers of causing a public nuisance by falsely promising that "home ownership of guns increases home safety and security." The Court of Common Pleas for Hamilton County disagreed and dismissed the case. Judge Robert Ruehlman wrote:

> In this case, the city has alleged that the defendants intentionally and recklessly marketed, distributed, and sold guns that they knew would be possessed and used illegally. An activity that is authorized by law cannot be a public nuisance

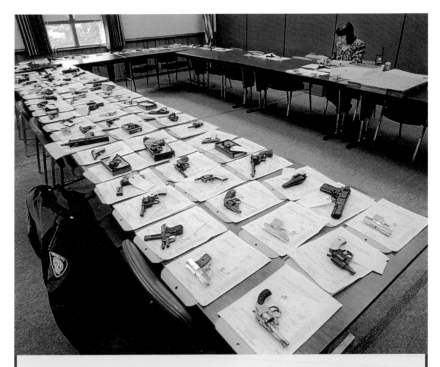

Although the Second Amendment calls for an armed citizenry, many states are actively trying to reduce the number of guns on the streets. Here, a program exchanging guns for grocery certificates netted over a hundred guns.

or absolute nuisance. . . . This is especially true where a comprehensive set of legislative acts or administrative regulations governing the details of a particular kind of conduct exist. . . . In sum, the city has no claim for public or absolute nuisance arising from the defendants' heavily regulated distribution of firearms, because 'what the law sanctions cannot be said to be a public nuisance.'[7]

The decision was upheld by the appeals court, which ruled, "Using a shotgun approach in its complaint, the city has made its broad assertions without alleging a direct injury caused by a particular firearm model or its manufacturer. We hold that the city's attempts to stand in the shoes of its citizens and to recover municipal costs must fail."[8]

Is it fair for a city that has not outlawed guns to sue gun manufacturers for selling guns to its citizens?

In a blow for the gun industry, the Ohio Supreme Court reversed the Court of Common Pleas, ruling that Cincinnati could proceed with its case. The majority opinion affirmed that, as a direct result of the misconduct of gun manufacturers, the City of Cincinnati had suffered the "actual injury and damages including, but not limited to, significant expenses for police, emergency, health, prosecution, corrections and other services" that the city had alleged in its complaint.[9] (A dissenting opinion was published, but it dissented on points of law unrelated to the substance of the complaint.)

The suits expose a possible rift between the gun industry and traditional advocates of the right to bear arms. Unlike the NRA, gun manufacturers may be willing to tolerate limited control policies—such as increasing waiting periods and background checks—in order to ensure a lawsuit-free future and a stable marketplace. Gun dealers would actually benefit from tighter controls on private sales and transfers at gun shows. Trading tighter restrictions for a reduction in liability might be a smart move: Some of the civil lawsuits are demanding hundreds of millions of dollars in damages. The $2 billion industry has much smaller coffers than the powerful tobacco companies, which have withstood similar lawsuits and paid hefty damage awards.

Gun manufacturers and owners' groups argue that manufacturer liability lawsuits are logically flawed because people who misuse guns bear full responsibility for their actions. They also say the suits endanger a legitimate industry. Gun manufacturers have defeated some attempts by cities and individuals to hold them liable for gun violence, and have had success in persuading many state legislatures to pass laws blocking suits of this type. However, they have had some setbacks at the state level, too, and it is not clear if this year's Congressional session will pass the proposed Protection of Lawful Commerce in Arms Act. It appears possible that gun manufacturers may be willing to accept some restrictions in exchange for a reduction in liability, but those who support gun owners' rights remain unlikely to compromise.

> **Who should pay the cost of treating gunshot wounds for people without insurance?**
>
> **Should knife manufacturers be financially responsible for knife wounds?**
>
> **If so, then should there be distinctions among manufacturers of steak knifes, butter knives, and hunting knives?**

The Future of Gun Control in the United States

Scaling Back Gun Control: The Bush Administration

When the Republican staff of President George W. Bush moved into the offices occupied by two-term Democratic President Clinton, both sides of the gun control debate knew change was on its way. Sure enough, one of the new administration's first moves was to vocalize its view on the Second Amendment.

In a letter to the NRA, Attorney General John Ashcroft wrote, "the text and the original intent of the Second Amendment clearly protect the right of individuals to keep and bear firearms." He continued, "Like the First and Fourth Amendments, the Second Amendment protects the right of 'the people,' which the Supreme Court has noted is a term of art that should be interpreted consistently throughout the Bill of Rights."[1]

Ashcroft's statement embraced the individual-rights interpretation of the Second Amendment. It went against the grain of national precedent set by the Supreme Court in *United States v. Miller* and embraced the more radical view espoused by the Fifth Circuit in *United States v. Emerson.* Gun rights groups celebrated Ashcroft's signals that the tide was changing in the White House. Supporters of gun control, of course, worried that their mission would become harder to accomplish.

> **Is it odd that John Ashcroft supports individual rights in the case of guns, when he has spoken against abortion rights and called for giving police greater leeway to tap phones?**
>
> **What does this suggest about the nature of the debate over the Second Amendment and gun control?**

The NRA has placed the repeal of major gun control measures at the top of its agenda for the 21st century. Chief among its targets are the Assault Weapons Ban and some provisions of the Brady Act. The Assault Weapons Ban will expire in 2004 unless Congress and the President renew the law. The NRA has already begun pressuring representatives to let it fade away.

The NRA would also like to see limits imposed on the background checks performed under the Brady Act. Under current Department of Justice regulations, records of background checks conducted by the National Instant Check System (NICS) must be kept for 90 days. In July of 2001, the General Accounting Office (GAO), which monitors governmental spending for Congress, reported that "during the first six months of the current 90-day retention policy, the FBI used retained records to initiate 235 firearm retrieval actions, of which 228, or 97 percent, could not have been initiated under the proposed next day destruction policy."[2] Attorney General John Ashcroft proposed a policy under which records of background checks through the NICS, a part of the Brady Act, would be destroyed after one business day.

Gun control supporters say such a policy would prevent law enforcement officials from identifying gun buyers who slip

Lawsuits against gun manufacturers allege that manufacturers deliberately make weapons that are useful for crime and market these weapons to criminals. In the case of assault weapons, the anti-control argument tends to shift from self-defense–based argumentation toward legal or theoretical argumentation. Many moderate groups agree that access to firearms like these should be strictly regulated.

through the cracks and are approved for firearms purchases that they should not be allowed to make. The Department of Justice solicited comments on Ashcroft's proposal, and the comment period expired on September 4, 2001. No final rule had been issued by late 2002.

What is the reasoning behind destroying records that could be used to track criminals?

Is the reasoning valid?

What should be the position of the attorney general, whose function is to prosecute federal crimes, in this debate?

Michael D. Barnes, president of the Brady Campaign to Prevent Gun Violence, said, "The GAO has found that if the Ashcroft proposal went into effect, hundreds of criminals, terrorists, and other prohibited purchasers—potentially more than 300 a year—would be on our streets with guns, and law enforcement would have no information about these cases until the guns are used to kill, maim, and rob innocent Americans."[3]

More Loopholes Emerge

During the summer of 2002, a new problem with Brady Act background checks was exposed. According to a report from the GAO, nearly 3,000 domestic abusers purchased firearms between 1998 and 2001, passing through a glitch in records check systems.[4] (If the FBI is unable to complete the Brady background check within three days, the sale is allowed to proceed.) This provision was a compromise that helped move the original Brady Bill through Congress.

Investigators were forced to chase after the abusers and more than 8,000 other prohibited buyers who were allowed to buy weapons. More than a quarter of the cases involved people convicted of misdemeanor domestic violence offenses. Because of poor record keeping and other problems, it is difficult to access such records. The GAO study argues that federal authorities should be given as much as 30 days to research suspicious cases before a sale is approved, noting that a relatively small number of buyers would be affected. Some members of Congress have recommended, in contrast, shrinking the background check time to 24 hours in some cases.

> Is the compromise concerning background checks a balanced one, or does one side give up more than the other?

Arming Pilots to Protect Against Terrorism

In the immediate aftermath of the terrorist attack of September 11, 2001, gun control seemed to fade from public attention. The lawsuits against gun manufacturers were mired in the appeals process. Crime was on the decline. However, as the Bush administration and representatives in Congress sought solutions to protecting domestic security, the issue of access to

In the wake of the September 11 hijackings, a successful push was made to allow pilots to carry guns. United Airlines announced plans to arm its flight crews with non-lethal "stun guns." The potential dangers of allowing weapons of any kind in the cockpit of an airplane makes this one of the more heated political arguments to emerge since the attack.

firearms rose back to the surface. A coalition of airline pilot unions, members of Congress, and the NRA began clamoring for legislation that would allow airline pilots to carry handguns. A bill passed in the House of Representatives in July of 2002, and supporters expected a companion bill to the pass the Senate before the end of the year.[5]

The practice of allowing pilots to carry firearms aboard planes was common until the 1980s and wasn't outlawed until July of 2001.[6] Airline manufacturers say that modern aircraft can function safely despite any decompression caused by bullet holes in the fuselage. Of 90,000 pilots who would be eligible to carry a gun, according to the Air Line Pilots Association, only 25,000 to 30,000 would take the training and be deputized as gun-carrying "federal flight deck officers." While seeking to win support in Congress, the bill's supporters also hurried to convince the President, who initially opposed the idea.

Critics of the measure argue that guns in the cockpit could cause problems rather than solve them. They say pilots should be allowed to focus solely on flying their planes, instead of attempting to manage a deadly weapon at the same time. Supporters of the measure counter that trusting pilots with fuel-loaded jet liners is far riskier than arming them with guns. Casting doubt on the reliability of the air marshal program, which places armed government employees on some flights, they say arming pilots is the only sure way to protect passengers.

> **Would you feel safer flying on an airplane whose pilot was armed?**
>
> **Should anyone else on the flight be armed?**
>
> **What is the best way for passengers and/or crew to defend an airplane?**

Progress Is Still Slow

Although surveys consistently show that a majority of U.S. citizens favor some form of increased gun control,[7] the gun control lobby has yet to achieve major legislation. The problem seems to be that the public lacks the commitment and passion for the issue needed to force change. The tens of millions of gun owners in the United States are active participants in gun culture. They may be more motivated than gun control advocates to support their candidates and feed the coffers of their institutions.

Gun Prohibition May Be the Next Step

The coming years are likely to see a variety of new gun control proposals, including imposing background checks on transfers at gun shows, registering all guns and licensing all owners, raising the legal age for purchasing handguns from 18 to 21, requiring safe storage of guns, and limiting handgun purchases to one per month. A growing number of gun control advocates urge U.S. citizens to forsake compromise and diluted measures in favor of a nearly complete ban on all firearms or on all handguns. *The Los Angeles Times* was one of the first major media outlets to advocate such a move. The newspaper's editorial board outlined its opinion in an editorial dated December 10, 1993:

> **What are the likely outcomes of the coming gun proposals?**
>
> **Which proposals will please or anger which interest groups?**

> We are at a crossroads in our long, ambivalent relationship with guns. We can continue our largely futile, and very costly, efforts to screen out 'unfit' gun owners, increase the penalties for gun crime and step up security around a growing list of special facilities such as schools and government offices. Or we can dramatically alter the basis for private gun ownership. Rather than assuming, as we do, that all citizens are presumptively entitled to own a gun unless a government agency demonstrates otherwise (such as through a background check) we must, as a nation, move toward a very different model, one that presumptively bars private citizens from owning a firearm unless they can demonstrate a special need and ability to do so.

Since the early 1980s, many of the major gun control groups have shied away from advocating total bans on handgun ownership.

The Violence Policy Center's Josh Sugarmann was one of the first vocal gun control players to embrace the idea again:

> A single consumer product holds our nation hostage: the handgun. We live our lives in the shadow of the unparalleled lethality of these easily concealed firearms. This permanent state of fear has become so accepted that we rarely even acknowledge it. The United States' handgun industry eagerly exploits this fear, selling its products to a dwindling market. Handgun makers promise a concerned public that the best salve for their fear of crime is to arm themselves with the very weapons that threaten them. A wide range of pro-gun advocates—manufacturers, magazines, lobbyists, and individual gun owners—extol the virtues of the most recent models of handgun. Their claims are validated by television and movie images, where handguns are routinely portrayed as effective self-defense tools posing little risk to the user. Although these claims are not borne out by the facts, they live on.[8]

Is there such a thing as a total ban?

Would this include assault weapons? BB guns? Slingshots?

How "gunlike" would an object have to be to qualify?

Is a total ban a violation of any right?

Sugarmann accuses the gun control lobby, of which he is a member, of becoming so concerned with political expediency that it sacrificed the only valid tool for stemming gun violence in the United States.

Can Safer Storage Reduce Accidents?

Other gun control advocates, with the support of suburban and urban police, have begun to focus on the issue of safe gun storage. They advocate using trigger locks, devices that make it impossible to pull the trigger without a key. They also urge gun owners to store their firearms in locked cabinets or safes. These

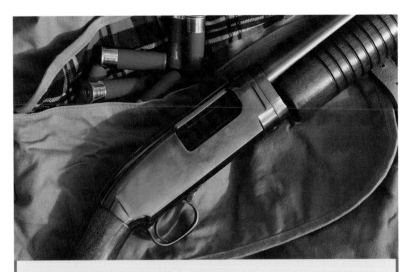

The debate over gun control generally is built on two bases: (1) the theory of it—whether the government has the power to regulate guns at all and, if it does, to what extent; and (2) the practice of it—the dangers inherent in giving many people access to powerful weapons. Although the idea of a total ban has recently re-entered the debate, this may not be reasonable, as powerful interest groups would oppose such a measure. But the questions of fear and public safety loom large, especially in the post–9/11 political climate.

safety measures focus on the tragic cases of accidental death when children find and play with their parents' loaded guns. The gun safety argument has led some people to believe that guns themselves should be designed to be less dangerous. Although groups such as the NRA oppose proposals that would set safe storage standards for firearm owners, gun manufacturers have begun to advocate the use of gun locks and similar devices.

Is Compromise Possible?

Social commentators who don't have a specific interest in limiting or increasing gun control offer insights that can't be found in the literature published by the differing sides. Many urge gun rights activists and gun control advocates to compromise, and they resurrect a long-stalemated debate. Others encourage both sides to advocate more politically distinct agendas.

Many commentators at both ends of the political spectrum think gun control fails to address the source of the United States' problems with violence and that a full-scale reevaluation of the nation's culture is needed to fix the broken parts. The columnist and author Anna Quindlen has said, in light of efforts to reduce violence in schools, "There is a lot of talk now about metal detectors and gun control. Both are good things. But they are no more a solution than forks and spoons are a solution to world hunger."[9]

> **A test is required before any person can be licensed to operate a car.**
>
> **Should people have to demonstrate their fitness to own guns?**
>
> **Or should the government have to disprove it?**

> **What can be done to make the United States less violent?**
>
> **Whose responsibility is it to make this happen?**

As the Bush administration seems prepared to limit gun control measures, new loopholes seem to emerge regularly in existing laws, and it is difficult for the gun control lobby to get new measures passed. Although the September 11 attack might be expected to have encouraged the public to support further limits on weapons, actually one result of the attacks was a new federal law permitting pilots to be armed for self-defense during flights. There is still talk of actually campaigning to ban guns entirely, but in the shorter term, safety measures like trigger lock requirements appear to have a stronger chance of passing. Meanwhile commentators speaking at a distance from the gun debate tend to ask whether the culture of violence in the United States is really the problem most in need of attention.

The Politics of Gun Control

1 Susan Schmidt and Ruben Castaneda, "U.S. Adds to Charges in Sniper Shootings; Affidavit Lists Evidence Found in Muhammad's Car," *The Washington Post*, October 30, 2002, p. A1.

2 Robert M. Thompson, Jerry Miller, Martin G. Ols, and Jennifer C. Budden, "Ballistic Imaging and Comparison of Crime Gun Evidence by the Bureau of Alcohol, Tobacco, and Firearms," National Integrated Ballistic Information Network (NIBIN) Program, BATF, U.S. Dept. of the Treasury, May 13, 2002, p. 2.

3 Brady Campaign, press release, Oct. 17, 2002, available online at *www.bradycampaign.org/press/release.asp? Record=434*; National Rifle Association, "Fact Sheet: 'Ballistic Fingerprinting': The Maryland Example: Costing Taxpayers Without Benefiting Law Enforcement," available online through *www.nraila.org*; New Jersey State Legislature legislative tracking site, "Second Reprint, Assembly, No. 438, State of New Jersey, 210th Legislature, As reported by Assembly Appropriations Committee on October 21, 2002, with amendments," *www.njleg.state.nj.us/2002/Bills/A0500/4 38_R2.PDF*.

Point: The Second Amendment Guarantees the Right to Bear Arms

1 John Adams, *A Defense of the Constitutions of Government in the United States of America* (1787–1788).

2 Cesare Beccaria, *On Crimes and Punishments* (*Dei delitti e delle pene*, 1764). Translation by H. Paulucci (1963), Prentice Hall, 1998.

3 Federalist Papers, No. 46.

4 Federalist Papers, No. 29.

5 Federalist Papers, Nos. 184–188.

6 Akhil Reed Amar and Alan Hirsch, *For the People: What the Constitution Really Says About Your* Rights, Simon & Schuster, 1998.

7 Albert Gallatin, letter to Alexander Addison, October 7, 1789. From Stephen Halbrook, *That Every Man Be Armed: The Evolution of a Constitutional Right*, University of New Mexico Press, 1984, p. 225.

8 *United States v. Verdugo-Urquidez*, 494 U.S. 259 (1990).

9 *United States v. Miller*, 307 U.S. 174 (1939).

10 *United States v. Emerson*, 270 F.3d 203 (5th Cir. 2001). The opinion, which includes a detailed pro-gun discussion of constitutional history, is available online at *www.ca5.uscourts.gov/opinions/ OpinHome.cfm*, filed under its revision date of November 2, 2001.

Counterpoint: Gun Activists Misconstrue the Second Amendment

1 Warren Burger, *The MacNeil-Lehrer NewsHour*, December 16, 1991.

2 Brady Center to Prevent Gun Violence, press release, October 17, 2001. Available online at *www.brady-campaign.org/press/release.asp? Record=353*.

3 Brady Campaign, press release, June 10, 2002, available online at *www.brady-campaign.org/press/release.asp?Record= 404*; Supreme Court Order List, June 10, 2002, available online at *www.supreme-courtus.gov/orders/courtorders/061002pzo r.pdf*; Haney v. United States, Petition for a Writ of Certiorari, 01-8272, Brief for the United States in Opposition, November 9, 2001, available online at *www.usdoj.gov/osg/briefs/2001/0responses /2001-8272.resp.html*; Emerson v. United States, Petition for a Writ of Certiorari, 01-8780, Brief for the United States in Opposition, November 9, 2001, available online at *www.usdoj.gov/osg/briefs/2001/ 0responses/2001-8780.resp.html*.

4 *Schenck v. United States*, 249 U.S. 47 (1919).

5 Harris Interactive, "The Harris Poll #26: The Gun Control Enigma," available online at *www.harrisinteractive.com/ harris_poll/index.asp?PID=89*; see also CNN, "Majority of Americans Favor Stricter Gun Control," *www.cnn.com/ 2000/ALLPOLITICS/stories/04/12/poll. guns.*

6 Michael A. Bellesiles, *Arming America: The Origins of a National Gun Culture*, Knopf, 2000.

7 Eric H. Monkkonen, *Murder in New York City*, University of California Press, 2001.

8 See Jon Wiener, "Fire at Will: How the Critics Shot Up Michael Bellesiles's book *Arming America*," *The Nation*, November 4, 2002, p. 28; press release, Emory University, October 25, 2002, available online at *www.emory.edu/central/ NEWS/Releases/bellesiles1035563546.html*; the report of the Emory investigation committee and Bellesiles' response and resignation, available on the same website; Michael Korda, "Loaded Words," originally printed in *Brill's Content*, February 2001, and reprinted on the NRA website; and *National Review Online* on the resignation, October 28, 2002, *www.nationalreview.com/seckora/ seckora102802.asp.*

Point: Gun Control Laws Reduce Violence

1 *U.S. National Center for Health Statistics, 2000.*

2 Frank Zimring and Gordon Hawkins, *Crime Is Not the Problem: Lethal Violence in America*, Oxford University Press, 1997.

3 Federal Bureau of Investigation, *Crime in the United States—1991 and 1997.*

4 Federal Bureau of Investigation, *Crime in the United States—2001*, available online at *www.fbi.gov/pressrel/pressrel02/cius2001.htm*. See also Federal Bureau of Investigation, *Crime Trends—2001, Preliminary Figures*, June 2002, available online at *www.fbi.gov/ucr/ 01prelim.pdf.*

5 John R. Lott, Jr., *More Guns, Less Crime: Understanding Crime and Gun Control Laws*, University of Chicago Press, 1998.

6 Violence Prevention Center, "Funder of the Lott CCW Study Has Links to the Gun Industry," *www.vpc.org/fact_sht/lottlink.htm*; John R. Lott, Jr., "All the News That Fits: Trigger Happy: Are the major media frivolous or biased? Some each, find our reporters in the field," *The National Review*, 22 June 1998.

7 Brady Center to Prevent Handgun Violence, *Concealed Truth: Concealed Weapons Laws and Trends in Violent Crime in the United States*, October 22, 1999.

8 All citations in this paragraph and the previous paragraph are from John Henry Sloan, Arthur L. Kellermann, et al., "Handgun Regulations, Crime, Assaults, and Homicide: A Tale of Two Cities." *The New England Journal of Medicine* 319:19(1988):1256.

9 The Brady Handgun Violence Prevention Act, Public Law 103–159, 1993.

10 Brady Center to Prevent Handgun Violence, July 27, 2000.

11 William J. Clinton, Speech at the Ohio Peace Officers Training Academy, February 15, 1994.

12 Marianne W. Zawitz, *Guns Used in Crime*, Bureau of Justice Statistics, July 1995, NCJ-14820, available online at *www.ojp.usdoj.gov/bjs/abstract/ guic.htm.*

13 U.S. Departments of Justice and Treasury, *Gun Shows: Brady Checks and Crime Gun Traces*, January 1999.

14 Marianne W. Zawitz, *Guns Used in Crime*, Bureau of Justice Statistics, July 1995, NCJ 148201, available online at *www.ojp.usdoj.gov/bjs/abstract/guic.htm.*

15 Josh Sugarmann, *Every Handgun Is Aimed at You: The Case For Banning Handguns*, The New Press, 2001.

Counterpoint: Gun Control Does Not Prevent Crime

1 William J. Vizzard, *Shots in the Dark*, Rowman & Littlefield, 2000.

2 Bureau of Justice Statistics, *Historical Statistics on Prisoners in State and Federal Institutions, Year End 1925–1986* and *Correctional Populations in the United States, 1987–1994*.

3 *See* NRA, "The Case for Repealing DC's Gun Laws," "The War Against Handguns," and "Ballistic Fingerprinting: The Maryland Example: Costing Taxpayers Without Benefiting Law Enforcement"; and Sandra S. Froman, "California Gun Vilification: A Blueprint for America," all available online through *www.nraila.org*.

4 Jens Ludwig and Philip J. Cook, "Homicide and Suicide Rates Associated With Implementation of the Brady Handgun Violence Prevention Act," *JAMA* 284:5 (2000):585.

5 Don B. Kates, "Gun Laws Around the World: Do They Work?" *The American Guardian* (October 1997):48–49, 60–62.

6 Gary Kleck and Marc Gertz, "Armed Resistance to Crime: The Prevalence and Nature of Self-Defense With a Gun," *The Journal of Criminal Law and Criminology* 86(Fall 1995):164.

7 John R. Lott, Jr., *More Guns, Less Crime: Understanding Crime and Gun Control Laws*, University of Chicago Press, 1998.

8 Gary Kleck, "Crime Control Through the Private Use of Armed Force," *Social Problems* 35(February 1988):15.

9 David B. Kopel, "Lawyers, Guns, and Burglars," *Arizona Law Review* 43(Summer 2001):345.

10 U.S. Department of Justice, Law Enforcement Assistance Administration, *Rape Victimization in 26 American Cities*, 1979, p. 31.

11 John R. Lott, Jr., *More Guns, Less Crime: Understanding Crime and Gun Control Laws*, University of Chicago Press, 1998.

12 John R. Lott, Jr., *More Guns, Less Crime: Understanding Crime and Gun Control Laws*, University of Chicago Press, 1998.

13 U.S. Department of Justice, National Institute of Justice, *The Armed Criminal in America; A Survey of Incarcerated Felons*, July 1985.

14 Gary Kleck, *Targeting Guns: Firearms and Their Control*, Aldine de Gruyter, 1997.

Point: Gun Manufacturers Should Be Held Financially Responsible for Gun-Related Deaths

1 Centers for Disease Control, National Vital Statistics Reports (NVSR) 49:8(September 21, 2001):10, available online at *www.cdc.gov/nchs/data/nvsr/ nvsr49/nvsr49_08.pdf*; NVSR 50:15 (September 16, 2002):10, available online at *www.cdc.gov/nchs/data/nvsr/ nvsr50/nvsr50_15.pdf*.

2 Allan Lengel, "The Price of Urban Violence," *The Washington Post* (December 28, 1997):B1.

3 Kenneth W. Kizer, Mary J. Vassar, et al., "Hospitalization Charges, Costs, and Income for Firearm-Related Injuries at a University Trauma Center," *JAMA* 273:22(1995):1768.

4 Wendy Max and Dorothy P. Rice, "Shooting in the Dark: Estimating the Cost of Firearm Injuries," *Health Affairs (Millwood)* 12:4(1993):171.

5 Kristen Rand, quoted in "New VPC Report Details How Liability Legislation (HR 2366) Would Protect Manufacturers of Guns Used in 1999 Columbine Massacre," The Violence

Policy Center, February 15, 2000. Available online at *www.vpc.org/press/0002dead.htm.*

6 Dina El Boghdady, "New Wal-Mart Policy Stiffens Requirements for Gun Sales," *The Washington Post* (July 4, 2002): E12.

Counterpoint: Gun Manufacturers Are Not Responsible for Gun-Related Deaths

1 John Lott, "Gun Shy: Cities Turn from Regulation to Litigation in Their Campaign Against Guns," *National Review* (Dec. 21, 1998):46.

2 Chris John, quoted in Robert A. Levy, "None of Their Business," *National Review Online* (*www.nationalreview.com/comment/comment-levy052202.asp*), May 22, 2002.

3 Brady Campaign, press release, Sept. 25, 2002, available online at *www.brady-campaign.org/press/release.asp?Record=4 26*; *Merrill v. Navegar, Inc.*, 26 Cal. 4th 465 (2001), Aug. 6, 2001.

4 Designated HR2037 and S2268.

5 See Dick Dahl, "The NRA Sees Room to Grow as Faithful Adjunct to the GOP," *The Nation*, November 4, 2002, p. 16.

6 Jeff Reh, Prepared Witness Testimony HR 2037, the Protection of Lawful Commerce in Arms Act. Subcommittee on Commerce, Trade, and Consumer Protection, April 18, 2002.

7 Robert Ruehlman, Court of Common Pleas of Ohio, *Cincinnati v. Beretta USA Corp. et al.*, 1999 WL 809838, 1 (Ohio Com. Pl. 1999).

8 Ralph Winkler, Court of Appeals of Ohio, First District Hamilton County, *Cincinnati v. Beretta USA Corp. et al.*, 2000 WL 1133078, 2 (Ohio App. 1 Dist. 2000).

9 Francis E. Sweeney, *City of Cincinnati v. Beretta USA Corp. et al.*, No. 2002-Ohio-2480 (Ohio, June 12, 2002).

The Future of Gun Control in the United States

1 John Ashcroft, letter to the National Rifle Association, May 17, 2001. Available online at *www.nraila.org/images/Ashcroft.pdf.*

2 General Accounting Office (GAO), *Potential Effects of Next-Day Destruction of NICS Background Record Checks*, July 2002. Available online at *www.gao.gov/new.items/d02653.pdf.*

3 Brady Center to Prevent Gun Violence, press release, April 11, 2001. Available online at *www.bradycampaign.org/press/release.asp?Record=393.*

4 U.S. General Accounting Office (GAO): *Potential Effects of Next-Day Destruction of NICS Background Record Checks*, July 2002. Available online at *www.gao.gov/new.items/d02653.pdf.*

5 For status, see *thomas.loc.gov/cgi-bin/bdquery/z?d107:HR04635:.*

6 Sally B. Donnelly, "Are We Ready for Pilots Packing Heat?" *Time Magazine*/Time.com, September 2, 2002.

7 See Ban Handguns Now, *www.banhandgunsnow.org.*

8 Josh Sugarmann, *Every Handgun Is Aimed at You: The Case For Banning Handguns*, The New Press, 2001.

9 Anna Quindlen, *Thinking Out Loud: On the Personal, the Political, the Public, and the Private*, Random House, 1993, p. 19.

General Resources

Cottrol, Robert J. *Gun Control and the Constitution: Sources and Explorations on the Second Amendment.* Garland, 1994.

Eggen, Dan. "Domestic Abusers Bought Guns." *The Washington Post,* June 26, 2002.

Henderson, Harry. *Library in a Book: Gun Control.* Facts on File, 2000.

John, Chris, quoted in Robert A. Levy, "None of Their Business," *National Review Online (www.nationalreview.com/comment/comment-levy052202.asp),* May 22, 2002.

Kleck, Gary, and Don B. Kates. *Armed: New Perspectives on Gun Control.* Prometheus Books, 2001.

———. *Point Blank: Guns and Violence in America.* Aldine de Gruyter, 1991.

———. *Targeting Guns: Firearms and Their Control.* Aldine de Gruyter, 1997.

———, and Marc Gertz. "Armed Resistance to Crime: The Prevalence and Nature of Self-Defense with a Gun." *Journal of Criminal Law and Criminology* 86(1995):150.

Kopel, David B, ed. *Guns: Who Should Have Them?* Prometheus, 1995.

———. *The Samurai, the Mountie, and the Cowboy: Should America Adopt the Gun Controls of Other Democracies?* Prometheus, 1992.

The Los Angeles Times, editorial, December 10, 1993.

Quindlen, Anna. *Thinking Out Loud: On the Personal, the Political, the Public, and the Private.* Random House, 1993.

U.S. Government Accounting Office: *Potential Effects of Next-Day Destruction of NICS Background Record Checks,* July 2002 (*www.gao.gov/new.items/d02653.pdf*).

Vizzard, William J. *Shots in the Dark.* Rowman & Littlefield, 2000.

Zawitz, Marianne W. "Guns Used in Crime." Bureau of Justice Statistics, July 1995, NCJ-14820.

U.S. Treasury: Bureau of Alcohol, Tobacco, and Firearms: ATF Online
www.atf.treas.gov
Includes reports on crime trends, as well as a great deal of other information essential to the debate; its report on "ballistic imaging," also called "ballistic fingerprinting," is available at *www.atf.treas.gov/nibin/0502nibinrpt.pdf.*

Library of Congress: THOMAS: Bills in the News: Guns
thomas.loc.gov/home/textonly.html#gun
The premier source for updates on pending firearm legislation.

U.S. Sentencing Commission
www.ussc.gov
Includes detailed figures on federal crimes and sentencing.

Centers for Disease Control (CDC) National Center for Health Statistics
www.cdc.gov/nchs/fastats/firearms.htm
Offers statistics on mortality involving firearms.

U.S. Department of Justice (DOJ): Bureau of Justice Statistics
www.ojp.usdoj.gov/bjs/cvict.htm
Offers figures on crime victimization.

U.S. House of Representatives: Transcript and Prepared Testimony, Hearing on HR 2037, the Protection of Lawful Commerce in Arms Act, House Committee on Energy and Commerce, Subcommittee on Commerce, Trade, and Consumer Protection, April 18, 2002.
energycommerce.house.gov/107/hearings/04182002Hearing537/hearing.htm
energycommerce.house.gov/107/action/107-94.pdf
These materials contain arguments for and against a bill that would ban lawsuits against gun manufacturers over the criminal use of firearms.

Federal Bureau of Investigation (FBI): Uniform Crime Reports
www.fbi.gov/ucr/ucr.htm
Among the most thorough and most reliable sources of statistics on crimes of all kinds.

Pro–Gun Control

Cook, Philip J., and Jens Ludwig. *Guns in America: Results of a Comprehensive National Survey on Firearms Ownership and Use.* The Police Foundation (*www.policefoundation.org*), 1996.

———. *Gun Violence: The Real Costs.* Oxford University Press, 2002.

———. "Litigation as Regulation: The Case of Firearms," Terry Sanford Institute of Public Policy, Duke University, Working Papers Series SAN01-09, March 2001. Available online at *www.pubpol.duke.edu/people/faculty/cook/SAN01-09.pdf.*

Kellermann, Arthur L., Frederick P. Rivara, et al. "Suicide in the Home in Relation to Gun Ownership." *New England Journal of Medicine* 327:7(1992):467.

———, Frederick P. Rivara, et al., "Gun Ownership as a Risk Factor for Homicide in the Home." *New England Journal of Medicine* 329:15(1993):1084.

Rand, Kristen, quoted in "New VPC Report Details How Liability Legislation (HR 2366) Would Protect Manufacturers of Guns Used in 1999 Columbine Massacre," report of the Violence Policy Center, released February 15, 2000. Available online at *www.vpc.org/press/0002dead.htm*.

Sloan, John Henry, Arthur L. Kellermann, et al., "Handgun Regulations, Crime, Assaults, and Homicide: A Tale of Two Cities." *New England Journal of Medicine* 319:19(1988):1256.

Sugarmann, Josh. *Every Handgun Is Aimed at You: The Case For Banning Handguns.* The New Press, 2001.

American Bar Association Coordinating Committee on Gun Violence

www.abanet.org/gunviol/

A section of the American Bar Association's website presenting a moderate pro-gun control position. A useful links page connects to archives of court decisions, material on gun laws and regulations, organizations with varying positions, and descriptions of gun control policies outside the United States.

The Brady Campaign to Prevent Gun Violence

www.bradycampaign.org

One of the strongest voices in the debate over gun control. Advocates strongly for gun control but also provides some neutral information, such as congressional voting records, summaries of current and pending legislation, and material on laws by state. See also the Campaign's sister organization, the Brady Center to Prevent Gun Violence (*www.bradycenter.org*).

The Million Mom March

www.millionmommarch.org

Has merged with the Brady Center and Brady Campaign. Named for an anti-gun march of 750,000 people in Washington, D.C. on Mother's Day of 2000.

The Brady Center's Legal Action Project

www.gunlawsuits.org

The litigation arm of the Brady Center. Provides litigation updates and legal arguments in favor of gun control.

The Violence Policy Center

www.vpc.org

A major proponent of gun control, possibly more intensely opposed to firearms in general than is the Brady Center/Brady Campaign.

Join Together Online

www.jointogether.org/home/

A project of the Boston University School of Public Health working to reduce substance abuse and gun violence.

Ban Handguns Now

www.banhandgunsnow.org

A project of the Violence Policy Center that favors a complete ban on handguns.

Bowling for Columbine (2002), **Michael Moore**

This film is critical of gun advocates and the NRA but does not see gun control laws as a complete answer to the problem of U.S. gun violence. Moore implicates self-perpetuating interracial fear as part of the larger cultural problem.

Stray Dog (1949), **Akira Kurosawa**

This film offers an interesting perspective, removed in place and time, on some elements of the present-day gun control debate, including the issues of illegal handgun dealing and ballistic "fingerprinting."

Anti–Gun Control

Amar, Akhil Reed. "The Bill of Rights and the Fourteenth Amendment." *Yale Law Journal* 101(1992):1193.

Ashcroft, John. Letter to the National Rifle Association, May 17, 2001. Available online at *www.nraila.org/images/Ashcroft.pdf*.

Halbrook, Stephen. *That Every Man Be Armed: The Evolution of a Constitutional Right*. University of New Mexico Press, 1984.

Kates, Don B. "Handgun Prohibition and the Original Meaning of the Second Amendment." *Michigan Law Review* 82(1983):204.

Levinson, Sanford. "The Embarrassing Second Amendment." *Yale Law Journal* 99(1989):637. Also anthologized, with other thought-provoking cases and law review articles, in Cottrol, *Gun Control and the Constitution: Sources and Explorations on the Second Amendment*.

Lott, John R., Jr. *More Guns, Less Crime: Understanding Crime and Gun Control Laws*. University of Chicago Press, 1998.

Malcolm, Joyce Lee. *To Keep and Bear Arms: The Origins of an Anglo-American Right*. Harvard University Press, 1994.

Poe, Richard. *The Seven Myths of Gun Control: Reclaiming the Truth About Guns, Crime, and the Second Amendment*. Prima, 2001.

Van Alstyne, William. "The Second Amendment and the Personal Right to Arms." *Duke Law Journal* 43(1994):1236.

Volokh, Eugene. "The Commonplace Second Amendment." *New York University Law Review* 73(1998):793.

The National Rifle Association

www.nra.org

Perhaps the center of the anti-control side of the debate. Offers many pro-gun arguments, position papers, legislative updates, links to articles, and much more.

The National Center for Policy Analysis

www.ncpa.org

An multi-issue conservative think tank that takes detailed pro-gun positions.

GunCite: Gun Control and Second Amendment Issues

www.guncite.com

Covers the anti-control side of the argument thoroughly and enthusiastically.

The Journalist's Guide to Gun Policy Scholars and Second Amendment Scholars

www.gunscholar.org

This list of scholars who are "skeptical of gun control" by Prof. Eugene Volokh of UCLA Law School gives not only specialties and contact information, but also useful lists of publications and some links to matter such as congressional testimony. A separate page on the site gives a politically broader selection of links to organizations and information on the topic, though it is still more or less weighted against gun control.

Legislation and Case Law

United States v. Cruikshank, 92 U.S. 542 (1875)

In this post–Civil War case, the Supreme Court refused to find that a group of white racists in Louisiana had broken the law by "banding together" to violate the rights of two men "of African descent and persons of color," including not only their rights to vote, assemble, and enjoy equal rights and freedoms under the laws, but also specifically their claimed Second Amendment right "to keep and bear arms for a lawful purpose." The Court wrote, "The right . . . of 'bearing arms for a lawful purpose' . . . is not a right granted by the Constitution. Neither is it in any manner dependent upon that instrument for its existence. The Second Amendment declares that it shall not be infringed; but this . . . means no more than that it shall not be infringed by Congress." The NRA sees this language as saying that "the right of the people to keep and bear arms was a right which existed prior to the Constitution." However, the decision's more general effect was to say that victims of organized intimidation could only turn to their state and local governments, not to the federal government, for protection. In the 20th century, the Supreme Court gradually found that most of the Bill of Rights applies, via the Fourteenth Amendment, to the behavior of state and local officials in addition to the federal government. Together, Congress and the courts made clear that the federal government protects civil rights such as the right to vote and the right to equal protection of the laws. However, the Court still has not explicitly stated whether the Second Amendment applies to state and local official action.

Presser v. Illinois, 116 U.S. 252 (1886)

Upheld the conviction of Herman Presser for riding through the streets of Chicago at the head of a 400-man armed company that did not have government permission to assist in the national defense. The Court stated: "It is undoubtedly true that all citizens capable of bearing arms constitute the reserved military force or reserve militia of the United States as well as of the States, and in view of this prerogative of the general government, as well as of its general powers, the States cannot, even laying the constitutional provision in question [the Second Amendment] out of view, prohibit the people from keeping and bearing arms, so as to deprive the United States of their rightful resource for maintaining the public security, and disable the people from performing their duty to the general government." The NRA argues that this case also suggests the Second Amendment applies to the actions of state and local governments; the Brady Center's Legal Action Project disagrees.

Miller v. Texas, 153 U.S. 535 (1894)

"[D]efendant claimed that the law of the state of Texas forbidding the carrying of weapons, and authorizing the arrest, without warrant, of any person violating such law, under which certain questions arose upon the trial of the case, was in conflict with the second and fourth amendments to the constitution of the United States. . . . We have examined the record in vain, however, to find where

113

the defendant was denied the benefit of any of these provisions, and, even if he were, it is well settled that the restrictions of these amendments operate only upon the federal power, and have no reference whatever to proceedings in state courts."

The National Firearms Act of 1934 (NFA)

Imposed a tax on the manufacture and sale of machine guns, silencers, and short-barrel (sawed-off) shotguns and rifles and made registration of manufacture and importation mandatory; purchase or other transfer required a background check by the FBI and the approval of local officials.

The Federal Firearms Act of 1938

Required annual licensing of dealers and banned sale of guns to known criminals.

United States v. Miller, 307 U.S. 174 (1939)

Held that the National Firearms Act (NFA) was not unconstitutional, either as an impingement by the federal government on rights reserved to the states or as a violation of the Second Amendment. A sawed-off shotgun has no "reasonable relation to the preservation or efficiency of a well-regulated militia," and possession of one is not a right guaranteed by the Second Amendment.

Haynes v. United States, 390 U.S. 85 (1968)

Held that a criminal cannot be convicted for failing to register a firearm because of his Fifth Amendment right against self-incrimination—that is, it is illogical to penalize a person who is in unlawful possession of a firearm for not registering that firearm.

The Gun Control Act of 1968 (GCA)

Banned gun ownership by members of many classes of people, including drug addicts, minors, convicted felons, and people with mental illness; required serial numbers on all guns; banned commerce in guns and ammunition through the mail; set the minimum purchase ages of 21 for handguns and 18 for "long guns"; banned the importation of foreign military products, Saturday Night Specials, and some semi-automatic weapons; required licensed dealers to keep records of transactions and authorized the federal government to inspect those records as well as the dealers' inventories.

United States v. Cody, 460 F.2d 34 (8th Cir. 1972)

Ignorance of the law is no excuse for acquiring a firearm from a dealer through intentional false statements, and the federal law banning such actions is constitutional.

United States v. Swinton, 521 F.2d 1255 (10th Cir. 1975)

A person not licensed as a dealer in firearms who sells a firearm can be convicted under a state statute even if the sale is not part of a full-time occupation or done for profit.

United States v. Warin, 530 F.2d 103 (6th Cir. 1976), *cert. denied*, 426 U.S. 948 (1976)

Held that the fact that a state citizen is subject, like other citizens of that state, to enrollment in a state militia does not justify that citizen's possession of a submachine gun. "It is clear that the Second Amendment guarantees a collective rather than an individual right."

The Arms Export Control Act of 1976 (AECA)

Invests the president with the authority to control the importation and exportation of "defense articles" through permits and licenses; prohibits commerce in such articles with "proscribed countries."

United States v. Oakes, 564 F.2d 384 (10th Cir. 1977), *cert. denied*, 435 U.S. 926 (1978)

Affirmed that the Second Amendment does not guarantee the right to possess an unregistered firearm with no proven connection to a state militia, even if the possessor himself is affiliated nominally with a state militia. Neither a Kansas state law specifying that the state militia included all "able-bodied male citizens between the ages of twenty-one and forty-five years" nor the possessor's affiliation with a nongovernmental "militia-type organization" justified possession.

Lewis v. United States, 445 U.S. 55 (1980)

Held that prohibitions contained in the Gun Control Act of 1968 against the possession of firearms by convicted felons were not unconstitutional. Reaffirmed *Miller*: "[T]he Second Amendment guarantees no right to keep and bear a firearm that does not have 'some reasonable relationship to the preservation or efficiency of a well regulated militia.'"

Quilici v. Village of Morton Grove, 695 F.2d 261 (7th Cir. 1982), *cert. denied*, 464 U.S. 863 (1983)

Upheld the constitutionality of a local ordinance banning handgun possession entirely in the city of Morton Grove, Illinois.

The Firearms Owners Protection Act of 1986

Allowed interstate sale of rifles and shotguns between parties who meet in person and comply with the laws of both states. Increased some penalties for criminal sale or use of guns and banned commerce in machine guns by private citizens. However, this law has been criticized by the Brady Campaign for having increased the number of gun sales without background checks, "opened up the 'gun show loophole'," and made the inspection and prosecution of lawbreaking firearms dealers more difficult.

The Gun-Free School Zones Act of 1990

Generally prohibited the possession and/or discharge of a gun in a school zone; allowed for certain practical exceptions.

United States v. Verdugo-Urquidez, 494 U.S. 259 (1990)

Primarily a Fourth Amendment case, but seen by the NRA as reinforcing the idea that the Second Amendment's use of "the people" refers to an individual right.

United States v. Hale, 978 F.2d 1016 (8th Cir. 1992)

Held that the Second Amendment does not protect individual possession of military weapons. Reaffirmed the power of Congress to regulate trade in firearms as a form of interstate commerce.

The Brady Act of 1993

Required implementation of a system of background checks of prospective purchasers of handguns (in states that had not already passed such legislation). However, affected not all firearm transfers but only sales by licensed dealers.

The Violent Crime Control and Law Enforcement Act of 1994

Aimed at reducing the trafficking of semiautomatic assault weapons; banned various models. Prohibited gun ownership by anyone under a restraining order for domestic violence; raised the standards for procuring a license to sell guns; prohibited generally the sale of handguns to minors and any traffic in magazines that held at least ten rounds of ammunition.

United States v. Lopez, 514 U.S. 549 (1995)

In a 5-to-4 vote, struck down the Gun-Free School Zones Act of 1990 as beyond the limits of congressional power to regulate interstate commerce.

The Domestic Violence Offender Gun Ban of 1996

Prohibited anyone convicted of a misdemeanor for a domestic offense from owning a firearm.

Printz v. United States, 521 U.S. 898 (1997)

Restricted the application of the federal Brady Act by finding that the federal government could not require state and local law enforcement officials to conduct background checks under the Act.

United States v. Emerson, 270 F.3d 203 (5th Cir. 2001) *cert. denied by Supreme Court Order List of June 10, 2002*

Upheld the conviction of a man who illegally possessed a gun while under a restraining order for domestic violence, but also said the Second Amendment supports an individual right to gun ownership. Supported the domestic violence law in the case as among the "limited, narrowly tailored specific exceptions or restrictions" that the Second Amendment could reasonably permit. The text of this opinion is available online at *www.ca5.uscourts.gov/opinions/OpinHome.cfm*, filed under its revision date of November 2, 2001.

United States v. Haney, 264 F.3d 1161 (2001), *cert. denied by Supreme Court Order List of June 10, 2002*

Upheld a law banning private ownership of machine guns. The text of this opinion is available online at *www.kscourts.org/ca10/cases/2001/08/00-6129.htm*.

The Our Lady of Peace Act (HR4757, 2002)

Passed the House of Representatives in the fall of 2002 under the pressure of the sniper serial killings in the area of Washington, D.C.; named for a church that was the site of a double murder. Would improve background check mechanisms to make them more effective in identifying people with criminal records who should not be allowed to purchase firearms.

Concepts and Standards

"a well-regulated militia"

individual right v. collective right

manufacturer liability

assault weapon

Saturday Night Special

targeted ban

Beginning Legal Research

The goal of POINT/COUNTERPOINT is not only to provide the reader with an introduction to a controversial issue affecting society, but also to encourage the reader to explore the issue more fully. This appendix, then, is meant to serve as a guide to the reader in researching the current state of the law as well as exploring some of the public-policy arguments as to why existing laws should be changed or new laws are needed.

Like many types of research, legal research has become much faster and more accessible with the invention of the Internet. This appendix discusses some of the best starting points, but of course "surfing the Net" will uncover endless additional sources of information—some more reliable than others. Some important sources of law are not yet available on the Internet, but these can generally be found at the larger public and university libraries. Librarians usually are happy to point patrons in the right direction.

The most important source of law in the United States is the Constitution. Originally enacted in 1787, the Constitution outlines the structure of our federal government and sets limits on the types of laws that the federal government and state governments can pass. Through the centuries, a number of amendments have been added to or changed in the Constitution, most notably the first ten amendments, known collectively as the Bill of Rights, which guarantee important civil liberties. Each state also has its own constitution, many of which are similar to the U.S. Constitution. It is important to be familiar with the U.S. Constitution because so many of our laws are affected by its requirements. State constitutions often provide protections of individual rights that are even stronger than those set forth in the U.S. Constitution.

Within the guidelines of the U.S. Constitution, Congress—both the House of Representatives and the Senate—passes bills that are either vetoed or signed into law by the President. After the passage of the law, it becomes part of the United States Code, which is the official compilation of federal laws. The state legislatures use a similar process, in which bills become law when signed by the state's governor. Each state has its own official set of laws, some of which are published by the state and some of which are published by commercial publishers. The U.S. Code and the state codes are an important source of legal research; generally, legislators make efforts to make the language of the law as clear as possible.

However, reading the text of a federal or state law generally provides only part of the picture. In the American system of government, after the legislature passes laws and the executive (U.S. President or state governor) signs them, it is up to the judicial branch of the government, the court system, to interpret the laws and decide whether they violate any provision of the Constitution. At the state level, each state's supreme court has the ultimate authority in determining what a law means and whether or not it violates the state constitution. However, the federal courts—headed by the U.S. Supreme Court—can review state laws and court decisions to determine whether they violate federal laws or the U.S. Constitution. For example, a state court may find that a particular criminal law is valid under the state's constitution, but a federal court may then review the state court's decision and determine that the law is invalid under the U.S. Constitution.

It is important, then, to read court decisions when doing legal research. The Constitution uses language that is intentionally very general—for example, prohibiting "unreasonable searches and seizures" by the police—and court cases often provide more guidance. For example, the U.S. Supreme Court's 2001 decision in *Kyllo v. United States* held that scanning the outside of a person's house using a heat sensor to determine whether the person is growing marijuana is unreasonable—*if* it is done without a search warrant secured from a judge. Supreme Court decisions provide the most definitive explanation of the law of the land, and it is therefore important to include these in research. Often, when the Supreme Court has not decided a case on a particular issue, a decision by a federal appeals court or a state supreme court can provide guidance; but just as laws and constitutions can vary from state to state, so can federal courts be split on a particular interpretation of federal law or the U.S. Constitution. For example, federal appeals courts in Louisiana and California may reach opposite conclusions in similar cases.

Lawyers and courts refer to statutes and court decisions through a formal system of citations. Use of these citations reveals which court made the decision (or which legislature passed the statute) and when and enables the reader to locate the statute or court case quickly in a law library. For example, the legendary Supreme Court case *Brown v. Board of Education* has the legal citation 347 U.S. 483 (1954). At a law library, this 1954 decision can be found on page 483 of volume 347 of the U.S. Reports, the official collection of the Supreme Court's decisions. Citations can also be helpful in locating court cases on the Internet.

Understanding the current state of the law leads only to a partial under-standing of the issues covered by the POINT/COUNTERPOINT series. For a fuller understanding of the issues, it is necessary to look at public-policy arguments that the current state of the law is not adequately addressing the issue. Many groups lobby for new legislation or changes to existing legislation; the National Rifle Association (NRA), for example, lobbies Congress and the state legislatures constantly to make existing gun control laws less restrictive and not to pass additional laws. The NRA and other groups dedicated to various causes might also intervene in pending court cases: a group such as Planned Parenthood might file a brief *amicus curiae* (as "a friend of the court") — called an "amicus brief" — in a lawsuit that could affect abortion rights. Interest groups also use the media to influence public opinion, issuing press releases and frequently appearing in interviews on news programs and talk shows. The books in POINT/COUNTERPOINT list some of the interest groups that are active in the issue at hand, but in each case there are countless other groups working at the local, state, and national levels. It is important to read everything with a critical eye, for sometimes interest groups present information in a way that can be read only to their advantage. The informed reader must always look for bias.

Finding sources of legal information on the Internet is relatively simple thanks to "portal" sites such as FindLaw (*www.findlaw.com*), which provides access to a variety of constitutions, statutes, court opinions, law review articles, news articles, and other resources — including all Supreme Court decisions issued since 1893. Other useful sources of information include the U.S. Government Printing Office (*www.gpo.gov*), which contains a complete copy of the U.S. Code, and the Library of Congress's THOMAS system (*thomas.loc.gov*), which offers access to bills pending before Congress as well as recently passed laws. Of course, the Internet changes every second of every day, so it is best to do some independent searching. Most cases, studies, and opinions that are cited or referred to in public debate can be found online — and *everything* can be found in one library or another.

The Internet can provide a basic understanding of most important legal issues, but not all sources can be found there. To find some documents it is necessary to visit the law library of a university or a public law library; some cities have public law libraries, and many library systems keep legal documents at the main branch. On the following page are some common citation forms.

COMMON CITATION FORMS

Source of Law	Sample Citation	Notes
U.S. Supreme Court	*Employment Division v. Smith*, 485 U.S. 660 (1988)	The U.S. Reports is the official record of Supreme Court decisions. There is also an unofficial Supreme Court ("S.Ct.") reporter.
U.S. Court of Appeals	*United States v. Lambert*, 695 F.2d 536 (11th Cir. 1983)	Appellate cases appear in the Federal Reporter, designated by "F." The 11th Circuit has jurisdiction in Alabama, Florida, and Georgia.
U.S. District Court	*Carillon Importers, Ltd. v. Frank Pesce Group, Inc.*, 913 F.Supp. 1559 (S.D.Fla.1996)	Federal trial-level decisions are reported in the Federal Supplement ("F.Supp."). Some states have multiple federal districts; this case originated in the Southern District of Florida.
U.S. Code	Thomas Jefferson Commemoration Commission Act, 36 U.S.C., §149 (2002)	Sometimes the popular names of legislation—names with which the public may be familiar—are included with the U.S. Code citation.
State Supreme Court	*Sterling v. Cupp*, 290 Ore. 611, 614, 625 P.2d 123, 126 (1981)	The Oregon Supreme Court decision is reported in both the state's reporter and the Pacific regional reporter.
State statute	Pennsylvania Abortion Control Act of 1982, 18 Pa. Cons. Stat. 3203-3220 (1990)	States use many different citation formats for their statutes.

page:
11: © Corbis
19: Associated Press, AP
49: © Corbis
57: © Philip James Corwin/Corbis
59: © Bettman/Corbis
68: © Steve Starr/Corbis

74: Associated Press, AP
83: © Owen Frankel/Corbis
89: Associated Press, AP
91: Associated Press, AP
96: © Paul Edmondson/Corbis
98: Associated Press, AP

44, 70, 72, 80: Adapted from the U.S. Department of Justice: Federal Bureau of Investigation (FBI): *Crime in the United States 2001* (Uniform Crime Reports), October 28, 2002. Document available online at *www.fbi.gov/ucr/cius_01/01crime2.pdf.* The document defines *justifiable homicide* (p. 72) as "[t]he killing of a felon, during the commission of a felony, by a private citizen."

63: Adapted from U.S. Department of Justice: Federal Bureau of Investigation (FBI): Uniform Crime Reports: Supplemental Homicide Reports, 1997, special tabulation prepared by Northeastern University, Boston, Massachusetts. Reprinted in U.S. Department of the Treasury and U.S. Department of Justice, *Gun Crime in the Age Group 18–20,* June 1999. Document available online at *www.ustreas.gov/press/releases/reports/report.pdf.*

76: Adapted from U.S. Department of the Treasury: Bureau of Alcohol, Tobacco, and Firearms (ATF): *Crime Gun Trace Reports (1999),* November 2000. Document available online at *www.atf.treas.gov/firearms/ycgii/1999/genfindings.pdf.*

ANGELA VALDEZ lives in Philadelphia, Pennsylvania. A graduate of New York University, she has reported for several newspapers, including *Newsday*, *The Flint Journal*, and *The Philadelphia Inquirer*. She is now working toward her Ph.D. in U.S. history at the University of Pennsylvania.

ALAN MARZILLI, of Durham, North Carolina, is an independent consultant working on several ongoing projects for state and federal government agencies and nonprofit organizations. He has spoken about mental health issues in over twenty states, the District of Columbia, and Puerto Rico; his work includes training mental health administrators, nonprofit management and staff, and people with mental illness and their family members on a wide variety of topics, including effective advocacy, community-based mental health services, and housing. He has written several handbooks and training curricula that are used nationally. He managed statewide and national mental health advocacy programs and worked for several public interest lobbying organizations in Washington, D.C. while studying law at Georgetown University.